The P̶ ̶ ̶ ̶ ̶ ̶ ̶ ̶.

How to Build Influence and Make an Impact as a Global Payroll Professional

BART VAN DER STORM

Acknowledgements

My special thanks go to my wife, who is my North Star and supports me in whatever I do. To Edwin Spaink, who has been my partner in crime in writing this book. And to my team, who have given me inspiration and continue to do so every day.

Table of Contents

Preface................................... 10

Introduction............................... 13
    If confidence doesn't come naturally to you......... 15
    The four C's............................ 17
    Setting the right expectations................. 20
    The Payrollmind DNA explained............... 24
    You don't need to be a lone wolf to succeed in payroll . . . 27

Part I

Chapter 01: The State of Our Industry............... 33
    The Problems Faced by Multinational Organizations . . . 33
    Why I Wrote This Book: A Journey to Success and Influence 34
    Seizing the Countless Opportunities: Developing the Appetite For Payroll................................. 36
    The Intricate Web That Is Payroll................ 37
    Becoming a Powerful Force for Good............. 38
    The Complexity of Payroll: A Puzzle with Countless Pieces 38

Chapter 02: Crossing Borders 41
    Common Issues 42
    The Deeper Problem. 45
    How to Win. 46

Chapter 03: Becoming a Payrollmind. 48
    Vision Matters 49
    Are Vision and Purpose the Same?. 50
    The Importance of Discovering Your Purpose 51
    Purpose and Performance. 52
    How Goal Setting and Purpose Work Together. 53
    Short-Term and Long-Term Goal Setting. 55
    Understanding the Game 57
    Storytime 58

Chapter 04: The First Step 60
    Taking That First Step 62
    The Mindset Shift 63
    The Robber of Dreams. 65
    The Great Lie 66
    A Fresh Start Each Month. 69
    Commitment. 71
    Beyond Values 74
    Focusing on What You Can Control 76
    Eliminate Distractions: They Poison Your Performance. . 78

Part 2

Chapter 05: Effective Communication 83
    What's Your Communication Style, and Why That Matters 84
    The High Cost of Poor Communication. 86
    Poor Communication Makes You Invisible and Ineffective 87

Why Finding Your Voice Matters............... 88
What Does Authentic Communication Look Like for a
|Payroll Professional?..................... 89
Cultural Dexterity (Cultural Competence)......... 91
Communicating with Stakeholders and Senior Leadership
For Stronger Partnerships................... 93
Self-Confidence and Effective Communication...... 98
How to Be Heard........................ 99
Emotional Intelligence and Empathy........... 100
Navigating Difficult Conversations through Effective
Communication....................... 102
Reflection Time.......................106

Chapter 06: Problem-Solving.................. 108
Transforming Challenges into Opportunities....... 109
The Mark of Self-Sufficiency and Independent Thinking 110
The Nature of the Beast....................111
The Sustainable Problem-Solving Process..........113
Evolving Excellence and Problem-Solving Skills..... 114
An Ethical Imperative......................115
Don't Avoid the Facts......................116
Strategies to Increase Your Level of Problem-Solving ...117
Technology, Automation, and Problem-Solving..... 118

Chapter 07: Growing Partnerships................ 122
The Painful Truth.........................123
The Difference between Your Team Member and
Your Work Partner........................125
Staying Focused on Your Goal.................127
Problem-Solving in Partnership.............. 128
Forging Strategic Partnerships................ 130

| 7

Chapter 08: Global Payroll Lifecycle 134
    Perspective Matters 135
    Global Payroll Lifecycle from Start to Finish 138
    The Twenty-Two Processes of the Global Payroll Lifecycle 141
    Claiming Your Seat at the Table 145

Chapter 09: Building Influence 149
    The Paradox of Influence 150
    Speak Up and Make Your Case. 151
    Authentically Vulnerable and Yet Impenetrable. 152
    Breaking Down Cross-Departmental Silos 154
    Navigating Office Politics while Building Influence 155
    Strategies for Building Influence 158

Part 3

Chapter 10: Overcoming Challenges 163
    The Resilience Factor 164
    Developing High Levels of Mental Endurance 165
    Obstacles Are Stepping Stones 166
    A Learner's Mind. 167

Chapter 11: Leadership as a Force for Good. 169
    Team Motivation: The Heart of Leadership 170
    Conflict Resolution 171
    Cultivating Leadership Qualities. 173
    The Pursuit of Continuous Education 174
    Leadership as a Force for Good. 175

Conclusion 177
   From Taker to Giver 179
   The Ever-Evolving Journey 181
   The Evergreen Legacy of Influence 182

Recommended Resources 183
   Payrollmind DNA assessment 183
   Strategy session. 183
   Payrollminds newsletter. 184
   Payrollminds LinkedIn 184

Preface

It was 2013 and I was living in Amsterdam. At the time, I was contemplating if global payroll truly was the career for me. I asked myself questions around the skills required to be successful, which roles to look out for and at which companies. There were no real go-to resources or mentorships. So how do I get from where I was to where I truly wanted to be? I found certificate programs focusing on the processes, governance and other much needed aspects of global payroll. I ended up getting those certificates, and later went on to rewrite them and deliver the courses around the world myself—but it wasn't easy. Oh no, it was a hard and, at most times, a very lonely journey. And something was missing; how to nurture and develop a payrollmind.

Little did I know that Bart, at the time, was already writing his story—just as I was. And now, years later we both find ourselves to be global payroll influencers based out of The Netherlands who have seen the world, and its cultural differences. If only there had been such an insightful and motivational persona like Bart to guide me in the right direction at the time. I know for certain that I would be a better leader, and global payroll professional, than I am now.

To be successful in global payroll (or in business in general) both Bart and I learnt that you need to put the people first, beyond titles and compensation packages. You are only as strong as the collective, and this collective starts with the global payroll team but also includes all actors in the end-to-end payroll process – you know who they are. Global payroll is an aorta of employee data and process; act like it. You must guide, enforce, or embrace when you need to, and always, always, inspire. Inspire others to bring the best version of themselves to (virtual) work, to see the bigger picture, and to get a little bit better everyday. This also means sharing not only your successes, but also your flaws, doubts, and uncertainties. Showing vulnerability is not a sign of weakness, it is a sign of strength – of development. Do not be a know-it-all, but be a beacon for others. Be balanced, be authentic – as wherever you go, you are the only person you bring with you.

Your career in global payroll is a marathon, not a sprint – building character, influence and charisma takes time to build, and grows over time into a payrollmind. Global payroll needs to challenge the status quo of how it has always been done, to fix what is said to be 'unbroken', and we need to start now – so should you. This transcends technical skills, know-how and business acumen; this requires deep interpersonal progression on the deepest levels. You need to outgrow the storyline of looking at others to change, not truly partnering to grow the collective. By doing something for a key figure within the organization, you can see the changes your team needs, and become a true partner for the business, and your main stakeholders.

If you find yourself in times of trouble, Bart speaks to you in this book through his deeply personal anecdotes. Whether you want to start or progress your global payroll career, find a better balance in work and life, reset your passion and mission, or better understand the payroll function within your organization, you'll be guided by the golden nuggets in this book.

You would be wise to read and fully internalize what Bart has to say, and connect with him personally in this book; a unique, must-have resource in the global payroll world. If only I had it back in 2013, I would want to go back to the future. So I guarantee you; you need it, just as I did, and still do.

MAX VAN DER KLIS

Introduction

Have you ever wondered what the secret sauce is behind some of the most remarkable men and women you've admired all your life? For me, that would be guys like Michael Jordan, Tiger Woods, and Elon Musk, and women like Oprah and even my wife. These are all people I greatly respect and admire—people I look up to still. And yet, I don't see myself any less than any of them because I've realized one thing about winners: there's a common thread the greats all seem to have in massive quantities, and that is *confidence*. Confident people are their own special kind of conquerors. You can place them in any industry, situation, or circumstance with the highest levels of adversity; sooner or later, they will come out on top.

The most successful people I know have very high and healthy doses of confidence that stem from knowing who they are. And, you see, I've always had that in abundance. I was recently asked how I got this way and what makes me, well, me. Upon reflection, I realized it's just who I am. I've always had a strong sense of my worth, values, and power. I view the world through the lens of being the hero of my story. I own my choices, good and bad, never shy away from responsibility, and above all else, I believe in myself. Can you unshakably say the same of yourself? If you can't or are hesitant to because you don't want others to think you are a jerk or too full of yourself, therein lie the root problems to your career.

You've been convinced the current struggles are due to your company, role, or other external forces, but in truth, the deficiency originates from the inside. If there's a singular message or golden nugget to be extracted from the ensuing pages, it would be this: You can only have what you dream of if you're willing to become more of your authentic self. Not some superficially made-up image that society or authority figures expect. Certainly not a version you think others would find more pleasing and appropriate. When you become who you are and show up in your role as that individual, things must change for the better. Until then, binge on as many YouTube videos as you like, fill your bookshelves with more career advice books, and listen to as many podcasts as you want; otherwise, you'll still struggle to have the career and life of your dreams.

Success and confidence go hand in hand.

If you lack authentic confidence, all the hard work in the world won't get you very far. And whether you're choosing to skim through or actually study this book, I can promise you one thing: this won't be some 'feel-good' motivational book for payroll professionals. If you're looking for a rush of adrenaline and some sweet-sounding words that get you high for a day before you jump back into that mundane reality that you're trying to escape, this book isn't for you. My bold, brutally honest personality is the reason I've built a thriving career over the past several decades in an industry that barely receives the recognition it deserves. Most people think of payroll as a dead-end career where people without dreams and ambitions land after being demoted. *How often have you or someone you know thought of payroll as a step down from something bigger?* It's not uncommon for me to hear payroll managers say their future feels dim and uncertain.

The fact of the matter is that I landed in this industry almost by accident, and I made it my mission to give it my all and win. And I've been winning ever since. I've worked with some of the biggest names in the business industry (think Cisco, Uber, and on and on). In all my years of corporate work, I've been running global payroll with the same mentality athletes have when going after a championship. The teams I've managed understood the meaning of hard work and dedication. If you expect me to sugarcoat things and tell you it was fun and stress-free, I'm sorry. Global payroll is a demanding and taxing job, a complex process that requires insane hours, a can-do attitude, and the kind of relentlessness you often see in the jungle. Well, I brought it all, and never in my watch did I let anything fall through the cracks. Month after month, with every payroll cycle, in a team of, at times, over a hundred people, we would focus on completing the mission. When you think about your current role and the organization you work for, how much of that secret sauce are you bringing to the table? Do you even know how to activate your secret sauce?

If confidence doesn't come naturally to you

For many of my readers, confidence and boldness don't come easy. There are layers of insecurities that have developed over time, maybe since childhood, that make it hard to show up as your authentic self. Perhaps you never took the time to figure out who you are, in which case many of the ideas in this book could feel very intrusive and harsh at first. I'd like to say I'm sorry for the moments where you'll feel offended by something I share, but that wouldn't be my truth. It takes a while to move past the first sting of interacting with me and my teachings, or so I've been told. I've got enough self-awareness to recognize that, admittedly, I may come across as too assertive; some might say aggressive, depending on your cultural background. That is exactly why I've covered the concept of communication styles in the chapter on effective communication, because you're going to need that kind of awareness too.

Why? Well, confidence isn't just about how you show up. It's also about being aware of how others receive you. The more aware you are, the easier it is to deal with their reactions. In this case, you're going through the words of a man who, by all accounts, deals straight, isn't afraid to call it like it is, and believes very much that your breakthrough in this space of global payroll requires you to step up your game and be bolder. That will stretch you. It will create all kinds of discomfort. I'm willing to go there if you'll stick with me through this journey.

After working with hundreds of talented professionals at my consulting firm and incubating some pretty extraordinary individuals who started out rather average yet now run global payroll for big brands like Netflix, I know confidence can be learned. It may come naturally to me and a few others, but even those who struggle with it can increase their self-worth and confidence levels with a little effort and the right mindset.

You might have picked up this book with the hopes that you'll finally get the technical solution to solve your current work issues, but I'm here to serve you the hard truth. Global payroll doesn't have a silver-bullet solution that will make it easy. The job is meant to be hard. Read that again. This role is hard. And that's a good thing because it helps mold you into a magnificent and highly valuable human being in the marketplace. You need to develop the right skills, mindset, and especially the confidence to go to battle each month and win. If that doesn't sound appealing, you might not be in the right industry.

The four C's

To succeed in global payroll, you need four things: confidence, competence, courage, and commitment. You must develop the ability to articulate your ideas, a deeper understanding of how to influence people so your difference-making initiatives come to fruition, and have an unyielding commitment to doing your best in any given situation so everyone gets what they want. None of these are inborn traits, nor do they solely depend on your formal degrees and technical skills. Yes, the technical skills do matter. And understanding the payroll process also matters. But if you're looking to create breakthroughs in your career and rise to the next level of freedom and success, you'll need a lot more than spreadsheet expertise.

Unfortunately, we must confront the harsh reality that, while every professional has the potential for tremendous success in their career, only a few will realize it. Many payroll professionals fall short, not due to poor organizational leadership or terrible bosses (though these factors can contribute), but rather because they lack the courage, commitment, and confidence to make critical decisions when the stakes are high and time is brief. That is the crux of the matter. It is the intangible qualities—the immeasurable stuff—that truly matter in those defining moments.

As a payroll professional, you know the cost of poor decision-making, particularly in critical moments, is catastrophic. Inefficiency and a lack of courage could result in someone not receiving their paycheck on time or, in some cases, at all. The consequences of such mistakes create a domino effect, ranging from missed mortgage payments to families going without food, depending on the severity of the error. All of this hinges on your ability to summon the courage to make the right choices when it truly matters. These high-stakes decisions lie at the heart of our profession. The weight of responsibility rests squarely on your shoulders, and the impact of your actions reverberates far beyond the confines of your office. It extends into the lives of individuals and families who rely on timely and accurate pay to meet their basic needs and secure their financial well-being.

The nature of our job leaves no room for half-heartedness or complacency. We win or lose. There is no in-between. And the consequences of our choices have real-life implications. It takes unwavering courage to navigate the complexities and constant flux of payroll management and make the right calls that uphold the financial stability of countless individuals. But courage alone is not enough.

Commitment is the fuel that propels you forward. It is your unwavering dedication to your craft and your relentless pursuit of excellence. Despite what you might think, mastering these intangible skills is not a matter of luck or sheer willpower alone. The dynamics at play in global payroll are intricate and multilayered. You are navigating different cultures and dealing with diverse perspectives, sometimes with different priorities. For instance, when we propose to "simplify payroll and make it better," the CFO might interpret it as a cost-cutting measure. At the same time, the HR director may see it as an opportunity to enhance employee engagement.

Meanwhile, the COO may prioritize effectiveness. All these viewpoints are valid, and yet unless we find a way to align them into a single agenda, it would be hard to build forward momentum. It's essential to recognize that payroll encompasses more than just processes and systems. As you'll soon discover when we unpack our framework of the payroll lifecycle in Part II of the book, learning to create alignment between the different building blocks essential to payroll success is a superpower you can acquire with a little effort and guidance.

Understanding this fundamental truth is the starting point for unlocking new opportunities. In this intricate web of global payroll, where numbers and spreadsheets dominate, lies an extraordinary chance for you, as a payroll professional, to transcend the boundaries of technical expertise. It is an invitation to embrace a higher purpose and become a powerful force for good within your organization and beyond.

Today, more than ever, it is vital for payroll professionals like you to tap into your potential, leverage your unique skills and abilities, and make a profound impact within your organization. This book is not another technical manual on the intricacies of payroll. While it will explore the essential foundations of our industry, it goes beyond mere numbers, charts, and formulas. It embarks on a transformative journey to equip any ambitious and determined payroll professional with skills and perspectives that will serve them throughout their career. These skills will enable them to make a significant difference within their organization and contribute to a better world.

Payroll professionals possess a privileged vantage point, as they have their fingers on the pulse of financial well-being, nurturing the lifeblood that sustains businesses and supports employees. Yet, the true extent of their influence is often underestimated. With every paycheck issued and every compliance hurdle overcome, payroll professionals shape the lives of individuals, families, and communities. They possess the potential to cultivate a culture of fairness, transparency, and empathy. As the future of work continues to evolve and globalize, the opportunities in payroll for those of us who aspire to make an impact and wield influence are expanding exponentially. Having spent twenty-five years in this industry, I am privileged to share the knowledge, insights, and solutions that could potentially redefine your career trajectory. This book encapsulates my best ideas on how to succeed. Consider it your guide to thinking outside the box and creating breakthroughs, both personally and professionally.

However, before we proceed, let's ensure there are no misconceptions about what this book can and cannot do for you.

Setting the right expectations

First and foremost, we must acknowledge that this book is not a magic wand that will instantly transform your career overnight. It is neither a shortcut to success nor a guaranteed formula for achieving all your professional aspirations. Instead, it is a roadmap that will provide you with invaluable insights, practical strategies, and thought-provoking exercises to help you navigate the complexities of the global payroll landscape. Throughout the pages of this book, I will share my experiences after almost twenty years in global payroll, working for Fortune 500 companies, and running my consulting firm. I've learned a lot along the way, made plenty of mistakes, risen to the top of the corporate ladder, and made even bigger mistakes. And just to ensure our journey together begins with the highest level of authenticity and integrity, let me state for the record: I'm not here to pretend that I know what it's like to be invisible or thought incompetent due to a lack of self-esteem or too much self-doubt.

These have never been maladies that plagued me. As far back as I can recall, I have always been a go-getter. I grew into a young, ambitious adult with dreams of creating massive success for myself, and I went into the payroll industry guns blazing. With each climb up the ladder, my work ethic, confidence levels, and success rate soared. Confidence, courage, commitment, and many of the qualities I discuss come naturally. Winning is my strong suit. But at what cost? That was the question I neglected to ask myself for many years until it was almost too late.

My focus at work used to be purely based on getting results and making sure the people who worked with me delivered. It was a brutal rise to the top, and I do not condone the process despite the fact that it did work for me in getting what I wanted. For many years, I was considered by many to be the guy who gets things done. I was the machine programmed to win at any cost. At times, the consequences of the collateral damage came at the expense of relationships I valued, but I kept going. All my talent and skills were internally focused and used only for personal gain. In other words, I was a taker until it got to a point where I consciously realized that I needed to make a drastic change and become a giver.

While this bold confession might repel some who read this book, it is my way of ensuring you get to see the journey of what it took to get me to become the payroll expert I am today. And I can assure you that today I am a very different payroll professional, dad, husband, friend, and leader because life forced me to a halt and compelled me to reflect upon the kind of leader I wanted to be in this space. So, at this point, you might feel as though we have nothing in common. Perhaps your struggles are due to a lack of confidence or feeling invaluable and unworthy. Or maybe you're struggling with knowing what you want to get out of this payroll career that seems to be hitting a dead end, but you don't know where to go next. Regardless of circumstances, shortcomings, or triggers, rest assured, there's something here for you.

As different as our stories might seem, the one thing we have in common is the burning desire to make something meaningful out of our lives, an ambition to be better than we are today. And—that dark season you're facing—we've all been there. I've been there. To the outside world, a die-hard attitude that creates success may not seem so ugly, but if you keep turning the pages, you'll see how even those of us with die-hard attitudes can get hit hard by life and find ourselves falling down the pit of despair. It is in those dark, terrible moments that we get to know what we're truly made of. In my case, that dark season where I lost everything was a defining moment that enabled me to consciously and intentionally put into practice the framework and mindset that you'll be uncovering in upcoming chapters.

Sometimes, things have to get really ugly before they become beautiful. Remember that.

Your ugly might differ from mine, but the burning desire for a better, more beautiful future is a shared goal. The principles that got me where I am are precisely what you need to turn your ugly into something magnificent. Many of my hard-learned lessons have become wisdom nuggets that others use to avoid pitfalls and build successful careers as payroll professionals. After training and mentoring hundreds of individuals directly and perhaps thousands indirectly, I'm now choosing to package some of that knowledge into this book.

My intention is to empower you with the knowledge and tools necessary to become an influential force within your organization. I firmly believe that you will be better equipped to drive positive change by enhancing your communication skills, developing your ability to influence others, and expanding your understanding of the broader organizational context.

But let me be clear: the responsibility ultimately rests with you. Your commitment, dedication, and proactive engagement with the concepts presented in this book will determine the extent of your growth and impact. It is a journey that requires self-reflection, continuous learning, and a willingness to step outside your comfort zone.

In the chapters that follow, we will explore a range of topics. From mastering effective communication techniques to understanding the power dynamics at play within your organization, each chapter will provide you with practical strategies and actionable advice. We will delve into the art of building influential relationships, navigating cultural differences, and aligning your goals with the broader objectives of your organization. Moreover, we will examine the intersection of global payroll and leadership, recognizing that, as a payroll professional, you possess unique insights and expertise that can contribute to the strategic direction of your organization. By embracing this broader perspective and adopting a proactive mindset, you will position yourself as a trusted advisor, a valued partner, and a catalyst for positive change.

I invite you to embark on this journey with an open mind, a thirst for knowledge, and a commitment to your own growth. Together, let's unlock the potential within you and unleash your power to become a positive force within your organization. Remember, this is not just about your success; it is about leveraging your skills and influence to create a ripple effect of positive change that extends far beyond your immediate sphere. By becoming a force within your organization, you have the opportunity to make a lasting impact on individuals, teams, and the overall organizational culture. But how do you transform from the current state to that desired vision of your best self living your best life? By cultivating the right mindset and making the Payrollmind DNA into your new standard operating procedure (SOP).

The Payrollmind DNA explained

Are you starting to feel stuck in your career? Maybe you're yearning for a breakthrough that propels you to new heights of success and fulfillment. If you're a payroll professional seeking to become a force for good within your department and organization, the Payrollmind DNA is the transformative model designed to empower you. It is a comprehensive framework that helps you integrate knowledge, mindset, and behavioral shifts to ensure holistic development and equip our students with the tools necessary to make a powerful and lasting impact within their organization. My consulting firm is established on the premise that we can empower both talented candidates and organizations to redefine the global payroll landscape. We aim to incubate a generation of self-sufficient payroll professionals, independent thinkers who are smart, courageous, focused, and on fire when it comes to solving the complex challenges of payroll—all while remaining agile. In short, we train, mentor, and inspire payroll professionals to become who they really are so they can deliver efficient, effective solutions quickly.

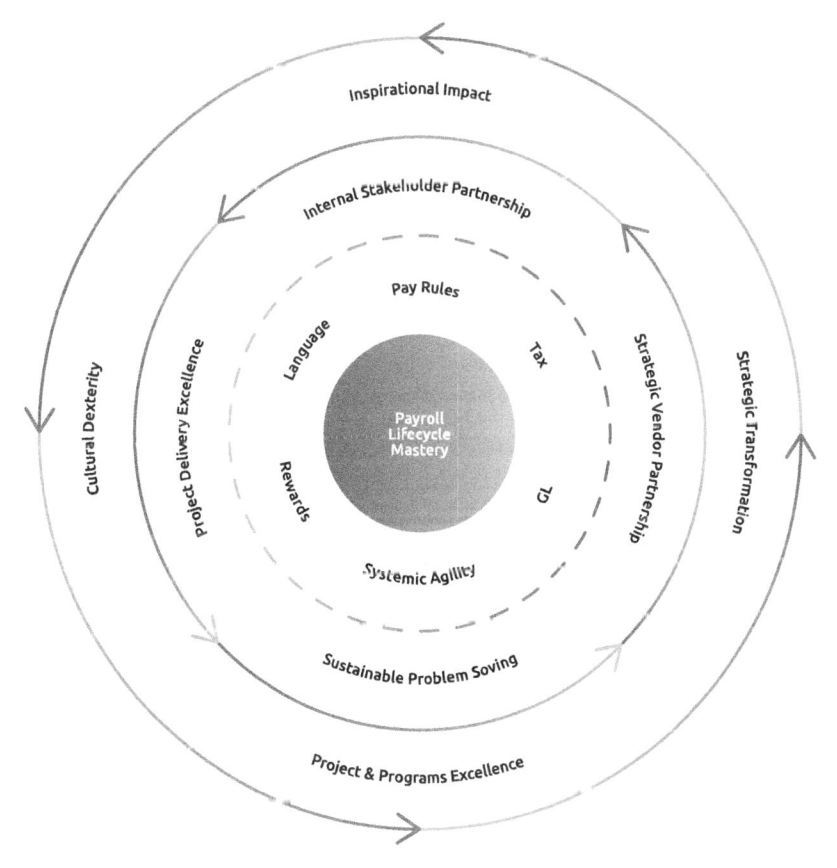

The payrollmind DNA competency framework.

Just like in golf, the journey begins with understanding your current "handicap" or skill level. For payroll professionals, it involves recognizing your strengths, weaknesses, and areas for improvement within your technical expertise, mindset, and behavior. This starting point, often referred to as your current handicap in golf, represents your current performance baseline.

As you take your first swing, you apply the knowledge and techniques acquired through your education and experience, much like leveraging your technical skills in payroll management. Just as a golfer strives to hit the ball accurately and navigate the course, you strive to execute your payroll responsibilities with precision and navigate the complexities of your role.

However, much like a golfer aiming to improve their game, you aspire to transcend the limitations of your handicap. You seek to elevate your performance, influence, and impact within your organization and beyond.

This is where our proprietary Payrollmind DNA model comes into play.

Just as a golfer continuously refines their swing and learns new strategies to conquer challenging holes, the Payrollmind DNA model equips you with the tools, strategies, and mindset to advance your knowledge, mindset, and behavior. It takes you beyond the complex, technical aspects of payroll and dives into the realm of soft skills that are essential for personal and professional growth. Just as a golfer seeks guidance from a coach or studies the techniques of professional players, you have access to the resources and guidance provided by the payroll DNA model at my global payroll consultancy. Visit *payrollminds.com* to learn more. Through customized assessments, exercises, and practical advice, you are able to fine-tune your communication, leadership, problem-solving, and other soft skills that amplify your impact. Each layer of the Payrollmind DNA presents you with new insights and practical techniques—much like the golfer progressing in improving his handicap. And just as the golfer's skills develop and their score improves, you experience a gradual transformation, moving from your current handicap to a higher level of mastery. As someone who loves playing amateur golf, my swing only improved when I worked with someone who could help refine my technique and mindset. Surprisingly, I witnessed the remarkable parallels between the game of golf and my personal and professional growth—and I hope you will, too. Although the intention in golf is to achieve a lower score as we strive to surpass present limitations, the purpose for you as you transcend present-day limitations will be to raise your score as a communicator, influencer, and leader. Anyone committed to making a positive change and doing meaningful work can only do so as they raise their score on these skills.

Through the Payrollmind DNA model, you can unlock your full potential, step by step, hole by hole, until you reach a point where your handicap no longer constrains you, but instead, you transcend to a higher level of excellence and become a force for good within your organization and the payroll industry as a whole.

You don't need to be a lone wolf to succeed in payroll

The demand for talent in our industry is high, but resources that can enable one to excel as a global payroll professional are scarce, making it hard for people entering payroll to know where to place their focus. Since no single curriculum will make you a masterful global payroll director, it can take time to map the journey to success. But even if your ambitions involve something other than becoming an executive in payroll, you still need proper education and development to execute your role with excellence. The Payrollmind DNA model recognizes that exceptional payroll professionals possess a unique blend of personal traits, mindsets, and acquired knowledge that shape performance. Formally acquired knowledge encompasses the technical competencies required to manage payroll effectively, such as data analysis, compliance, and system proficiency. On the other hand, mindset, beliefs, and personality traits are the intangible qualities that enable you to thrive in complex work environments, including communication, leadership, emotional intelligence, and critical thinking.

While technical skills can be acquired through education and experience, the right mindset and behavior are often more challenging to develop. Watching YouTube videos or reading blog articles on leadership and communication cannot instantly transform you into a great influencer or empathetic leader. It requires a deliberate and focused effort to apply these skills in real-life scenarios, adapt to diverse situations, and continuously improve.

The Payrollmind DNA model addresses this crucial aspect of professional development. It provides practical guidance and actionable strategies to help you master the soft skills that elevate your impact within your organization. By enhancing your ability to communicate effectively, build rapport, navigate conflicts, and inspire others, you become a powerful catalyst for positive change. Our sophisticated and multilayered model has been refined over the years, drawing from extensive research, industry best practices, and real-world experiences. We have witnessed its transformative power in countless payroll professionals who have transitioned from feeling undervalued and unseen to becoming influential leaders driving meaningful change.

In this book, I present my simplified version of the model—an accessible starting point that will set you on the path to personal and professional growth. Each chapter delves into key areas of development, offering concepts and reflective exercises tailored to enhance your knowledge and mindset while challenging some of your outdated beliefs. By engaging with these resources, you will uncover hidden potential, identify areas for improvement, and chart a course toward a brighter future. However, we can only go so deep in a single book before it becomes too technical. So, if you're intrigued by the high-level overview of the Payrollmind DNA approach presented across these pages and would like to learn more, I invite you to sign up for our free assessment. This assessment helps identify your payroll profile and uncover opportunities for growth. You'll also gain access to insights and tips from me and my hand-picked team of expert talent consultants. The time has come to break free from the constraints that have held you back. Unlock your full potential as a payroll professional, become a force for good within your organization, and shape the future of the payroll industry. The possibilities are endless, and the journey begins now.

Part I

Chapter 01:
The State of Our Industry

Global payroll, as an industry, is still in its infancy. As businesses expand their operations across borders, the need for streamlined and efficient payroll processes becomes increasingly vital. However, compared to other well-established disciplines, global payroll is relatively young. This presents an incredible advantage for forward-thinking payroll professionals like yourself who are willing to embrace the opportunities that lie within this burgeoning field.

The Problems Faced by Multinational Organizations

Organizations today encounter numerous challenges when it comes to managing global payroll. The complexities and intricacies of international regulations, varying tax systems, employee attraction and retention, hybrid work environments, and diverse employment laws can be overwhelming.

As a result, many organizations find themselves trapped in a web of convoluted processes and outdated systems, leading to inefficiencies, errors, and compliance risks. The need for a comprehensive and effective solution is more pressing than ever.

Why I Wrote This Book: A Journey to Success and Influence

Throughout my career, a recurring question from clients has echoed in my mind: "Bart, where can we find the best hire to handle these ten different roles we struggle with in payroll?" My answer has remained constant. Expecting excellence from an individual who is spread thin across multiple roles only leads to mediocrity, burnout, and costly errors. Yet, the blame often falls on the individual, labeling them as incompetent or lazy, when the real issue lies in the lack of clarity regarding their path to success.

I've experienced seasons in my life where I felt stuck, unfulfilled, and on the verge of burning out. As an employee in operations, I yearned to ascend to the next level but lacked the knowledge of how to grow. Similar to my golfing analogy, I was unaware of the steps required for progress. I believed working longer hours would suffice, only to exhaust myself without making any headway. Only when I took a step back and invested in my personal and professional growth did the insights I now share with you begin to take root in my mind.

Having transitioned from working for my father as a young teenager to working for Fortune 100 companies and eventually consulting for multinational organizations, I can confidently claim to understand the intricacies of designing and developing a successful career. The most important lesson I've learned is that it has little to do with acquiring more hard skills or seeking approval from superiors. Achieving a fulfilling and prosperous career that aligns with your desired lifestyle hinges on effective communication and securing buy-in from relevant stakeholders. It involves mastering the art of impact and influence, which cannot be taught in a classroom.

As I engage with payroll professionals across various industries today, I observe the same challenges I once faced. Should I change jobs or try to improve my current position within the company? Should I ignore the issues I identify in our processes since no one listens to me? Is self-employment the key to attaining more freedom? These are questions that have plagued me throughout my career, and I assure you that while it is natural to experience dissatisfaction, the true solution lies not in quitting or becoming indifferent but in developing the right qualities and fostering an atmosphere of influence that commands attention and genuine receptiveness to your ideas.

Consider this: Even if you were to leave your current job or join a different organization, what guarantees that you would find it easier to sway people's opinions and enact change? If you struggle to influence change in your current role, it is unlikely that a new position will yield different results. Yet, our industry is in dire need of transformation. To address the issues you have encountered, you must cultivate the ability to facilitate change. That is only possible if others perceive you differently. Let me guide you through this transformative journey and show you how to reshape others' perceptions of you, empowering you to achieve your own version of success. Together, we will navigate the path toward becoming an influential force within your organization and making a lasting impact on the payroll industry.

Seizing the Countless Opportunities: Developing the Appetite For Payroll

The impact of payroll on individuals, the company's financial stability, and the organization's compliance cannot be underestimated. It is a weighty responsibility that requires a deep sense of commitment and readiness to be at the forefront of such immense accountability.

Throughout my interactions with numerous individuals across the globe, I have come to realize that, despite our diverse backgrounds, we share a common thread. Whether I engage with a payroll professional in Asia, Australia, Europe, or America, the universal concern remains: ensuring timely and accurate employee payment. This unifying goal transcends cultural differences and binds us together.

Recognizing this shared objective, we must fulfill our responsibilities with unwavering integrity and determination. We are driven to seek innovative and improved approaches to the payroll process, aiming to overcome the significant challenges that impede our ability to deliver our best work. It is through this shared sense of purpose that we find the motivation to tackle the complexities of our profession head-on and strive for meaningful solutions.

The current landscape presents us with formidable obstacles that demand our attention. Cumbersome systems, convoluted procedures, and outdated practices hinder our progress, making it arduous to meet the standards we aspire to achieve. Yet, it is precisely these obstacles that inspire us to pursue new and better ways of doing things. We are driven by the desire to revolutionize the payroll process, streamline operations, and resolve the systemic issues that undermine our ability to excel.

In our quest for improvement, we acknowledge the significance of upholding our duty and delivering excellence in every aspect of payroll management. We recognize that our actions have a profound impact on the lives of individuals who depend on us for their livelihood.

Their financial well-being rests in our hands, and our commitment to meeting their needs is unwavering.

The Intricate Web That Is Payroll

In the pursuit of accurate and timely payroll, organizations often resort to patchwork solutions and manual workarounds. This approach creates a fragmented landscape where data is siloed, systems are disconnected, and collaboration between departments becomes arduous. As a payroll professional, you may have witnessed firsthand the frustrations caused by repetitive manual tasks, inconsistent data entry, and the constant need to reconcile discrepancies.

Furthermore, the lack of transparency and visibility hampers decision-making processes. Finance teams struggle to gain real-time insights, HR departments face challenges aligning payroll with employee benefits, and executive leaders find it difficult to track costs and manage budgets effectively. In such a dysfunctional environment, it's hard to tap into the full potential of the payroll function, hindering overall business growth and success.

Becoming a Powerful Force for Good

It is not enough to merely understand the problems faced by organizations. As payroll professionals, we must strive to become catalysts for change, using our expertise and influence to shape the future of our industry. Within the depths of my being lies a burning vision—a vision to see the payroll process simplified and payroll professionals empowered to unleash their full potential. It is a passion that has fueled my journey and shaped my purpose in life. The complexity of the payroll process and the unique challenges it presents in different countries and organizations have ignited a fire within me to drive change and revolutionize the way we approach payroll.

The Complexity of Payroll: A Puzzle with Countless Pieces

The intricacies of the payroll process are astounding. It is not merely a matter of calculating numbers and issuing paychecks; it is a labyrinth of regulations, policies, and systems that must be navigated with precision and accuracy. Each country has its own intricate web of tax laws, labor regulations, and reporting requirements, creating a complex tapestry that payroll professionals must unravel.

Furthermore, the diversity of organizations adds another layer of complexity. From multinational corporations with operations spanning multiple countries to small businesses with unique payroll needs, the intricacies multiply and the challenges become even more pronounced. Payroll professionals must deeply understand their organization's structure, policies, and intricacies to ensure compliance and accurate processing. In addition, we have to consider the drivers of your organization because different organizations will have different agendas driving goals and decision-making, which directly impact payroll process optimization and what's valued. Failing to understand what your organization considers a priority when attempting to improve your department can lead to disappointment since you will have difficulties aligning with senior leadership and gaining buy-in.

For example, I once witnessed a misalignment with an organization I was consulting for. The organization was preparing for an initial public offering (IPO), and senior leadership clearly outlined what they wished to focus on. Unfortunately, the guy running the payroll lacked the proper perspective to align his agenda and move in the same direction. He was passionately raising issues he wanted to solve, which had no bearing on what senior leadership had already announced as a priority. By the end of the meeting, he felt misunderstood and overlooked. But it wasn't entirely true. When senior leadership is focused on something like an IPO, telling them about how the company is losing a few thousand dollars on some unrelated policy isn't something they will prioritize.

So, it's essential to own your role and align with the organization. Embrace innovation and best practices that enable you to create greater leverage so you can meet your targets while still being a team player in the boardroom. It's not a matter of either or. Instead, it's about learning how to get what you want and still give the organization what they need.

In the chapters to come, we will embark on a journey that transcends traditional notions of payroll management. We will explore the multifaceted aspects of global payroll, delving into the technical foundations while simultaneously developing the soft skills necessary for success. This holistic approach will equip you with the tools, strategies, and mindset needed to become a powerful force for good within your organization and make a lasting impact in the payroll industry.

Chapter 02:
Crossing Borders

Global payroll is one of the more unique niches where navigating complex relationships amid a diverse range of cultures is actually the norm and comes as part and parcel of your daily role. As an individual born into a specific nationality and influenced by your culture, you interact with diverse colleagues within the payroll department and across various other departments. This multifaceted environment means you'll encounter people shaped by formal backgrounds (such as the distinct perspectives and priorities of HR leaders versus accountants) and cultural backgrounds (for example, the nuanced viewpoints and cultural nuances of an HR leader from Germany versus one from India).

This melting pot of differences contributes to how effectively we carry out our tasks to achieve departmental and company objectives despite our varying approaches and perspectives. In the world of global payroll, perspective holds immense significance. The more we broaden our perspectives, the better equipped we become to establish rapport, earn trust, and gain buy-in from individuals who may not share our appearance, thoughts, or actions. Expanding our perspective means we open ourselves to a wealth of opportunities. We gain insights into different ways of thinking, problem-solving, and decision-making. We learn to appreciate diversity's richness and understand that there are often multiple valid approaches to achieving a common goal.

Building rapport in a global payroll setting requires navigating through diverse cultural lenses. It involves understanding and respecting the cultural nuances that shape the perspectives and behaviors of our colleagues. The more we can acknowledge and value these differences, the easier it is to foster an environment of inclusivity, collaboration, and mutual understanding. Expanding our perspective also enables us to adapt to varying expectations and practices. It allows us to navigate complexities and find common ground when facing challenges. The ability to see beyond our own cultural biases and appreciate alternative viewpoints paves the way for effective communication, harmonious teamwork, and successful outcomes.

Common Issues

I once sat in a virtual meeting with people from around the world. We had someone from Germany, Japan, North America, Australia, India, and Brazil, and I'm from the Netherlands. Having all of these colleagues in a single virtual meeting meant that for some, it was the middle of the night; for others, early morning meant we required a keen and genuine desire to understand each other and have a productive meeting. So, as you can imagine, we are entering a meeting with different company titles, temperaments, biases, and vantage points.

Our style of communication is also extremely diverse. For example, Japanese and Indians always wait their turn to speak, whereas Dutch and Germans tend to speak loudly and boldly, which could often come across as aggressive and shouting. And although we all spoke English, the differences in accents meant some of us were harder to understand than others. Culture clashes are an inevitable reality. As professionals, we immerse ourselves in a dynamic environment where diverse cultures and geographies intersect. This collision of different perspectives, values, and communication styles can present unique challenges.

In my decades of traveling across the world and working with different groups, I've learned to be more mindful of my communication style and, at the very least, make sure that I circle back to my audience to ensure they received the message I was attempting to convey. When I am in Asia, I am more mindful and tweak my body language and tone of voice because I know that for many Asian cultures, my volume and style can easily come across as rude. And that's one of the things anyone working for global payroll needs to recognize because, without that level of self-awareness, the culture clash becomes a barrier that makes it impossible to get buy-in or support from the people who matter to you.

Another common issue that often arises between payroll and other departments is a lack of understanding of each other's skills and needs. Depending on your formal background and past experiences, you're likely more biased and prefer working with the department that aligns most with your frame of mind. For example, if you come from an accounting background, dealing with the finance team is easier than dealing with HR. But here's the thing: To do your job effectively and efficiently, you'll need to collaborate just as much with HR and any other team necessary to execute payroll on time. If you fail to recognize and appreciate that, practically speaking, the language HR will be most receptive to will differ from the approach the finance team prefers, then clashes and misunderstandings become inevitable. I like to use the example of Chinese, German, and Arabic individuals sitting at a table together, attempting to communicate with each other in their native language without a translator, and hoping to build rapport and gain an understanding of what the other parties desire while simultaneously attempting to get their point across.

Of course, that visual seems ridiculous because we know that no effective communication is possible where there are language barriers. First, the three people must find a way to understand each other's languages through a translator or by learning the language. In payroll, you speak a different "language" than HR or finance, so before effective communication and teamwork can become possible, you must find a way to understand each other's "language." What I find is that even though, as payroll, we might be in agreement with other departments about the problems that need to be resolved, clarity and communication must be prioritized because we all approach issues from different vantage points. Therefore, in order to align and execute the plan, we need better communication among ourselves.

Let me illustrate the subtle nuances that often get in the way of effective communication. Suppose I'm meeting with an Indian colleague from finance and his superior (the company's CFO). Most of the time, even if I ask him a direct probing question that he can answer, he will refrain from engaging because, in Indian culture, speaking up in front of a superior is frowned upon. In this case, I will get little to no proactive discussions with this colleague while the boss is in the room. Unfortunately, I may not get an answer from the CFO either because they may be embarrassed to acknowledge the problem. Now add to that equation that my bias might not be toward finance and spreadsheets but rather toward people and leadership, and we have an invisible wall that makes forward movement nearly impossible.

The Deeper Problem

As an individual and a payroll professional, you must start with yourself. Learn to recognize your biases and assumptions. Once you have more self-awareness, expand to learning more about the differences in cultural proclivities of the people in your department and across organizations.

One of the issues you must resolve is having clearly defined responsibilities and a clear understanding of what HR is, what payroll is, where the hand-offs are, and what their priorities are versus yours. The deeper problem, far beyond the complexity of the payroll process, is that few of us are willing to understand each other's priorities—let alone perspectives. But if we can get to a point where people are eager to develop that understanding, then we're halfway there, working better together and hitting our company goals. For example, it's one week to the deadline, and you, as a payroll professional, are more concerned about getting all the data accurately and on time so you can close payroll and move on to the next task. In contrast, the HR leader is more concerned about resolving the conflict between certain employees or ensuring you incorporate the bonuses promised to the employees because they keep asking for them. And it could just be that HR didn't send you the complete data that includes the bonus, but in their mind, you should still do it even if you didn't get the spreadsheets or data you requested on time. HR is more concerned about the negative impact on the people, and payroll is more concerned about the negative impact on the process. To the HR team, payroll seems to care more about the process than the people, but the payroll team knows that if the process is executed correctly, everyone will receive their compensation and bonus, so in the end, the people will be happy. But of course, that's often not how other departments observe it.

How to Win

The opportunity is for you to realize that every department, including your own, is made of individuals. And each individual possesses a unique vantage point and cultural biases that shape how they receive information. When dealing with cross-departmental colleagues, you want to have that at the forefront before you communicate your message or get the support you need. In an organization, everyone is attempting to hit their objectives, so their priorities may or may not be identical to yours. Still, if you do a great job implementing what you'll learn in the next chapter, you will find a way to find more common ground and alignment with others in the organization and their priorities. You'll start to develop the qualities that make you more influential. It's not about coercion or being the loudest person in the room. It's also not about forcing or pretending to care about others so you can have your way. You need to learn genuine understanding—always being curious enough when dealing with a member of your team or colleague in a different department who doesn't look, think, or act like you— so you can remain open to the possibility of finding a middle ground and building rapport.

To show you how little we know about each other and how much assumptions can get in the way, I'd like to end this chapter with a personal story of my experience years ago. I was in Japan for a business trip, and my company required me to hold extensive meetings with the payroll team. In the meeting rooms, the Japanese lady who ran the payroll was the most traditional Japanese woman you could imagine. She always bowed to show respect, hardly spoke unless spoken to, and never raised her voice. She was the quietest and most intelligent person in the room. My initial assumption was that she was a frail, feminine payroll leader. But I remained open and curious. And to my surprise, she proved me completely wrong. That same weekend, she invited me to lunch with her family, where I got to know her outside of the office walls and soon discovered that although she was running payroll, her family owned a race track, and she would spend her free weekend time racing Formula 1 cars on the track. A woman who initially seemed shy and frail was actually a badass with a need for speed.

Who knew? If I had allowed my assumptions to cloud my judgment, I would have missed building a genuine connection with a formidable colleague. There's a lesson in there for you.

Chapter 03:
Becoming a Payrollmind

Have you ever watched the movie *Ground Hog Day* with Bill Murray and Andie MacDowell? Some days, being a payroll professional can feel that way, too. And the reality for many in the industry is that it's not just the fact that you're always dealing with the same issues (inaccurate data, people not delivering on time, etc.); it's also that every month brings more issues than you can resolve. The to-do list is never-ending, the problems are constantly increasing, and often, you're like a firefighter moving from one burning forest to another.

Amid all this chaos, you need to think about your sanity. How do you stay focused, self- driven, and enthusiastic about doing your job with excellence? How do you protect your mental state?

After decades of experience in the trenches and mentoring numerous professionals, I firmly believe that developing a vision for your life is paramount. A compelling vision that pulls you forward is the best and most impactful way to shape your career and life. When I interview potential employees, whether for my own firm or for companies seeking to revitalize their payroll department, one of the first aspects I assess is the candidate's perspective. Does this person possess a solid vision? Do they have a clear sense of direction and a strong drive? Are they truly committed to building a thriving career, or will they falter when faced with challenges? I pay close attention to how well they articulate what they truly want.

The same questions apply to you because if you are genuinely dedicated to building a thriving career and becoming a force for good within your organization, it all begins with knowing yourself better. Understanding what you truly desire and where you envision yourself heading is essential. Another reality we must all acknowledge is that, while payroll is mission-critical for all organizations, it often fails to be seen as a priority. It is recognized as necessary, yet CEOs and department heads tend to prioritize their domains over the payroll function. As a result, the responsibility lies with you to take ownership of your career, role, and department. To do this effectively, we return to the topic of vision.

Vision Matters

What do we mean by vision? Vision is a clear, inspiring, and aspirational picture of the future. It is the mental image of what you want to achieve for yourself and your organization. A compelling vision serves as a guiding light, illuminating the path you must take to turn your dreams into reality.

Vision enables you to be clear about what you want and where you're headed, both personally and as a department. It also empowers you to navigate anything that blocks your progress, whether it's a bad review from a superior, a team conflict, or even issues that arise while dealing with other colleagues. I've witnessed a shift in behavior and career ownership where an individual who once struggled with interpersonal relationships at the office got hold of their vision. From that moment on, something just clicked. In a situation where they were being blamed for an issue that was clearly not their fault, instead of retaliating, they took ownership. They used it as an opportunity to demonstrate they were in charge and responsible for both good and bad results. This paradigm shift is only possible when one discovers a powerful guiding vision for one's life. And that's why finding your vision should matter to you, too. With vision and clarity, you can layer on the qualities of patience and relentlessness, which propel you to greater heights once activated.

Are Vision and Purpose the Same?

Vision and purpose are closely intertwined, but they have distinct focuses. Vision primarily relates to the future and the goals you aim to achieve. It is the "what" you aspire to accomplish, a destination you are working toward.

Purpose, on the other hand, is about the "why" behind your actions and goals. It is the deep and meaningful reason that drives you to do what you do. Purpose reflects your core values, beliefs, and the impact you want to create in the world.

While vision sets the direction, purpose provides the underlying motivation and meaning to your journey. Purpose acts as a compass, guiding you toward decisions and actions aligned with your values and sense of fulfillment.

If you're reading this and thinking, "I have no idea what my vision is, let alone my purpose,"... that's okay. About 80% of the payroll professionals whom I've met were exactly where you are. Many of us were conditioned into a mindset that doesn't promote deep conversations like finding one's purpose. We are taught to go to school, get a job, buy a car and house, start a family, etc. Few of us ever pause and take the time to understand whether that is what we really want. So, if this is the first time you're going to self-reflect and ask yourself some deep questions, congratulations. You have already taken the first step toward developing that Payrollmind DNA.

The Importance of Discovering Your Purpose

Everything we've discussed in this book thus far only becomes meaningful and possible if you connect with a deeper sense of purpose for your life. Finding your purpose is a transformative journey that can give your career a sense of direction. It involves understanding your values, passions, and unique strengths and aligning them with your work in the payroll profession. Consider the aspects of your job that bring you the most fulfillment and satisfaction. Is it the opportunity to contribute to employees' financial well-being or the ability to streamline processes and ensure accurate and timely payments? Identifying the alignment between your values and the purpose of your work will fuel your drive and provide a sense of meaning to your daily tasks.

Purpose and Performance

Understanding the strategic objectives of your organization is instrumental in discovering purpose. Explore how your expertise as a payroll professional can contribute to these goals and make a tangible impact. For example, you may realize that providing accurate and timely payroll services contributes to employee satisfaction, retention, and overall organizational success. By connecting your purpose to the organization's larger goal, you can derive a greater sense of fulfillment. When your work is aligned with your purpose, your performance reflects your passion and dedication.

Purpose fuels intrinsic motivation, allowing you to go above and beyond to deliver exceptional results. It provides a sense of meaning and fulfillment that transcends the day-to- day tasks of payroll management. With purpose as your driving force, you are more likely to set ambitious goals, take initiative, and continuously seek opportunities for growth and improvement. Problem-solving becomes part of your work DNA because your mind shifts from avoiding to embracing challenges as stepping stones toward your desires. The more you embody this presence of purposeful alignment, the more you inspire your colleagues and team members. Your enthusiasm and commitment create a positive work culture where everyone feels a sense of purpose and shared values. Purpose-driven professionals also tend to collaborate more effectively, as they are driven by a shared vision and a desire to achieve meaningful outcomes.

There will always be clearly defined targets where there is desire, purposeful alignment, and high performance. That's why, before we discuss goal setting and prioritization of your workload, we continually introduce the importance of reconnecting with your sense of purpose.

How Goal Setting and Purpose Work Together

Practical goal setting and purpose are deeply interconnected and work synergistically to drive personal and professional success. While purpose provides the overarching sense of meaning and direction, goal setting allows you to translate that purpose into tangled objectives and actionable steps. That's why famous coach and author Tony Robbins says, "Setting goals is the first step in turning the invisible into the visible." If you have dreams and a vision for a life you'd like, the way to realize that lifestyle will be through goal setting. Research in clinical and real-world settings has shown that goals can help us accelerate our personal growth and success. They keep us focused and accountable, allowing us to stay on the path that will lead to that meaningful, desirable life we wish to have. There's no better way to witness the power and impact of goal setting than in sports.

Consider the example of Michael Jordan, arguably the legend of NBA history. Jordan's exceptional career and multiple championship wins illustrate how goal setting and purpose are integral to achieving extraordinary success.

Jordan had a clear sense of purpose from the early stages of his career—to become the best basketball player in the world and win championships. His purpose was a driving force, guiding his dedication, work ethic, and commitment to continuous improvement. Jordan set ambitious goals to push himself beyond his limits and elevate his performance. These goals included improving specific skills like shooting, defense, and leadership and reaching milestones like winning NBA championships and earning individual accolades. He constantly raised the bar for himself, setting new challenges aligned with his purpose. His burning desire to win propelled him to give his absolute best on and off the court during practice sessions, regular-season games, or high-stakes playoff matches. His commitment to achieving his goals never wavered, even in the face of adversity. And let's be clear. Plenty of obstacles, challenges, and problems stood in the way of his wins. However, Jordan's goal-oriented mindset enabled him to maintain unwavering focus and mental resilience. He had the ability to block out distractions and maintain a laser-like focus on his goals, whether it was making a crucial shot, leading his team, or overcoming challenges. He remained mentally tough and embraced pressure-filled situations, harnessing the power of his purpose to drive his performance.

Does that mean he was perfect all the time? Of course not! In fact, he failed more than many of us ever will during our careers. Jordan famously said, "I've missed more than 9,000 shots in my career. I've lost almost 300 games … I've failed over and over and over again in my life. And that's why I succeed." That's a powerful statement to make. It demonstrates the power of having a clear purpose in life, strong intentions to be great, and clear goals that kept him on track even when things were hard. It took constant adjustment of his mind, his team's performance, and his own skillset to stay on the path of greatness. And that's one of the benefits that purpose and goal setting provide. They make it easier for individuals to assess where they are, adapt, evolve, and continually improve until the vision materializes.

It's easy to witness how unstoppable Michael Jordan was in the NBA during the 80s and 90s. We observe that focus, relentlessness, commitment, and drive, and we assume the wins came because of his talent. Sure, talent had something to do with it. Still, it took purpose and strategic goal setting to get him the legendary career he had. Jordan's success on the court is an inspiring example for individuals seeking to harness the power of purpose and goal setting to achieve remarkable accomplishments. I'm hoping you are that individual, and if I'm right, then it's time to get strategic about how you prioritize, adapt, and continually evolve yourself.

Short-Term and Long-Term Goal Setting

In the study on goal-setting theory published in 1968 by Edwin Locke, titled Toward a Theory of Task Motivation and Incentives, we find an eye-opening insight. Locke shares that having a conscious, purposeful goal increases the likelihood that your desired things will happen. In other words, setting goals that help you achieve what you want and creating definite, clear plans to help you get there increase your chances of success. How does this relate to your work? Consider, for a moment, the list of tasks or projects that feel like a headache.

You are likely to procrastinate or shortcut items on your to-do list that you don't feel like doing, although you know how critical they are to the organization. Often, we struggle to give our best each day because our brains are disengaged. There's no real reward for us, so we seek shortcuts or avoidance as much as possible. That doesn't make you a bad person, but it does lead to poor performance. The way to end this torturous existence is to be more proactive with goal setting. You must set personal long-term and short-term goals that excite you and tie them into the work KPIs or organizational objectives assigned to your role. Most people make the mistake of doing it backward. They look at what the organization wants them to do and then try to motivate themselves to show up on Monday morning feeling excited. That will only work for the first ninety days of a new job. Once the excitement or honeymoon effect wears off, you go back to hating your job, your boss, that b** from HR, and so on.

Let's not do this anymore. There is a better way, and this is it.

Start by identifying what you want (and I mean really want) in your life. Have a big, audacious goal that makes you come alive and aligns with your sense of purpose for living. Slice it down to short-term goals. Now, look at how you can tie the organizational duties and KPIs to those short-term goals. Knowing that you'll move closer to your larger goal and dream lifestyle as you hit those short-term goals—isn't that worth going to work next Monday?

This simple mindset shift will change how you approach tasks, problems, and your role. Do not short-change yourself by skipping over this part. The more clarity you have on your personal goals, the easier it will be to commit to higher performance and hitting the company targets.

Speaking of company targets, let's apply the same clarity principle. How clear are you and your team about the overall long-term company objectives? Have you broken down those long-term objectives to make them more manageable and easier to track? Does everyone on the team feel confident about their short-term objectives? Are they committed?

We'll discuss team alignment in a different chapter, but it does help to ensure that, at this point in our journey together, you recognize that goal setting is an exercise that begins with you and extends to your entire department.

Understanding the Game

At this point, the main thing to realize is that becoming a Payrollmind is less about titles, current limitations, and formal education and more about improving your mindset and believing in your untapped potential. The only way to improve or produce new outcomes is by unleashing something within you that hasn't been activated thus far. Usually, these hidden qualities and interpersonal skills lie dormant in all of us and often go unnoticed because they aren't as easy to label as the more technical skills. For example, it's easy to tell if you need a refresher on your Microsoft Excel skills. It's also easy to tell you need to learn a new tool because it speaks alien when you fire up the software. What's not so easy to tell is whether or not your interpersonal skills are weak. Or whether your emotional intelligence and empathy are low. Most of the time, you see the outcome of lacking the quality of empathy because each time you speak to Jenny from HR, things always escalate into a heated argument. You believe she's in the wrong, and you're just trying to get the data you need. But have you ever reflected on how she perceives you? Or what is your body language communicating?

The game of winning at global payroll requires that we develop enough self-awareness to reflect, question, and then activate certain subtle qualities that make it possible to do our job. And since our job is to intertwine with other people in other departments with different agendas and perspectives, our willingness to take initiative and learn to play the game as winners is nonnegotiable. So, if you want to make your career work in payroll and wish to have a thriving corporate career, keep turning the pages of this book because every ensuing chapter introduces one element essential to your global payroll playbook. And each of them is intended to help you finally play the game as a winner. It begins with "the first step."

Storytime

In my career, I can recall many people I started working with after being demoted or even made redundant from their previous organization. By going through the same concepts I'm sharing with you, they developed that Payrollmind DNA and transformed their career. For example, I worked with a great guy (let's call him Peter to protect his privacy) who was let go by his former organization because they didn't consider his role valuable. That was their mistake because, with a bit of ambition and the commitment, courage, consistency, and effort Peter put into his transformation, he forged an even better path as a payroll professional.

Today, he's leading the payroll team at one of the largest streaming platforms in the world.

I've witnessed many situations where an individual from a totally unrelated field was sent to payroll. Within a few years, that individual grew and became the lead of the department, not because they were an expert with numbers and spreadsheets but because they mastered all the other skills that actually make one excellent at handling global payroll. So, regardless of your current position and feelings toward the payroll function, if you have the desire and commitment to make it in this space, half the battle is won.

Chapter 04:
The First Step

Many years ago, while working at Cisco, my life took an unexpected turn when one of my children passed away. Suffice it to say that it was one of the darkest chapters of my life.

There were moments when I wasn't sure if my marriage would survive such a tragedy. I must admit, navigating that turbulent time with my wife and seeing how she grieved and handled herself made me appreciate, love, and admire her even more than before. My professional life took a hit. I felt myself hit rock bottom, both personally and professionally—not because there was something wrong at work—quite contrary, in fact. My organization and the bosses I reported to were most understanding and accommodating. My professional crisis was completely internal because my son's death had somehow disoriented my life compass, and I questioned everything. Known for my aggressive, go-getter approach, I had built a very successful career. I took no prisoners on my way to the top, and it had worked. Yet now, while wallowing in anguish and uncontrollable pain and lying face down at the bottom of my despair, the last thing I felt was successful.

I returned to work hoping to regain some sense of normalcy, but it quickly became apparent that I was no longer the same Bart van der Storm people knew. Somehow, my internal compass had shifted. The very job that I had enjoyed for years became unbearable.

Ultimately, I left a comfy job with an organization that had treated me well but no longer aligned with my newfound purpose. In many ways, the loss of my son broke me, and a part of me died with him, but in so doing, it gave rise to a new version of myself that proved to be better.

It took me a while to start rebuilding myself from the inside out. And often, I think back to how I was able to bounce back from that horrific chapter. The only answer that comes to mind is that I was *subject zero* to these concepts outlined in this book. I am the first success story of becoming a Payrollmind. And never were the ideas more helpful than when I needed to get back on my feet again and overcome the tragic loss of my son.

So, as you read this book, please don't assume we're only talking about financial or career success. These concepts will help you survive, thrive, or sometimes face even the most painful circumstances because, at the end of the day, your mind determines the quality of your life. A strong mind equals a strong life. A weak mind equals, well, you know the rest.

Taking That First Step

If you want to be in control of your career and life, you also need to be in control of your mind. Most people assume they need to control the uncontrollable. Growing up, I loved basketball and still do. I played all the way to the national level, and although I never made it to the NBA, I still treasure the lessons of the game that continue to apply to my life today.

One such lesson I'd like to share with you is knowing that although basketball is a team sport, you must be capable of carrying your own weight.

The more you train both mind and body, the easier it will be to implement the rules of the playbook and accomplish team objectives. Your coach may have a great playbook, and you might have a winning team, but if you're not willing to take that first step and develop your mind and physical state, you'll end up being the team's demise.

And that is where the rubber hits the road, so to speak. This career will always feel impossible until you commit to developing your mindset and skills (both hard and soft). Global payroll is a high-pressure, high-stakes, multilayered industry where problems are the norm. Combine that with the common issues that arise from dealing with different departments within the organization, and you're looking at a very demanding role—one that requires foresight, insight, high emotional intelligence, and the ability to discern the difference between what's urgent and important and what's not. I know I just made it seem impossible to thrive as a global payroll professional. Still, the truth is that a single move can simplify all this complexity—the decision to master oneself.

The more you know yourself, the easier it is to understand and know others. And the more self-awareness you have, the easier it becomes to show up as your authentic self, unapologetically. That means you understand your strengths, weaknesses, and quirks and find ways to complement and reinforce the areas needing improvement. But few of us take the time to learn ourselves, let alone identify our strengths and weaknesses. Unfortunately, that means that when interacting with others, we're likely to hit plenty of walls in an attempt to reach and influence the other. Let's work on that for a bit.

The Mindset Shift

What do your favorite athlete, business leader, actor, artist, and mentor have in common? In every instance, these individuals demonstrate mastery of their chosen craft. To do so, they've had to master their minds. The great Sun Tzu wrote in the book *The Art of War* that victorious warriors win first and then go to war, while defeated warriors go to war first and then seek to win. In other words, every battle is won before it is fought. That is the kind of mindset that champions possess. It's this mindset that frees you from average and mediocre results.

Because if you think about the words of Sun Tzu, you realize that it's not the tools, weaponry, strategy, or even size of the army that bring the win. Sure, you need all that. But you also need to have already won that battle before physically going to fight. And the only place humans have the power to do things (before physically enacting them) is in the mind.

The human mind is the most fascinating subject you could ever study. And you must, in fact, choose to study it to some degree—if only to understand yourself better. As a wise person once said, knowing thyself is the key to unknown joy, happiness, power, and peace. So, in addition to your strong work ethic, ambition, skills, years of experience, and natural talent, you will need to work on that mindset so it can propel you into greatness. A mind that is working for you is the best weapon, because then you become unstoppable. It doesn't happen on autopilot or by default, as most people assume. That's why Carol Dweck wrote the book *Mindset: The New Psychology of Success*, which I encourage you to add to your reading list. In her book, Dweck explores the concept of mindset and how it impacts our success and happiness in life. Dweck argues that people generally fall into two mindsets: a fixed mindset or a growth mindset.

A fixed mindset is the belief that our abilities and intelligence are fixed traits that cannot be changed. People with a fixed mindset tend to shy away from challenges, avoid failure at all costs, and view effort as a sign of weakness. They also tend to give up easily when faced with obstacles.

In contrast, a growth mindset believes that our abilities and intelligence can be developed through hard work, perseverance, and learning. People with a growth mindset embrace challenges, see failure as an opportunity for growth, and view effort as the key to mastery. They also tend to persist in the face of obstacles and setbacks.

Dweck argues that having a growth mindset is critical to success in all life areas, including education, career, relationships, and personal growth. By cultivating a growth mindset, individuals can overcome obstacles, learn from failures, and achieve their full potential.

The Robber of Dreams

We are here to unfold our full potential and live our best lives. That is only possible if one is willing to reexamine their beliefs and mindset and shift to cultivating a more growth-oriented state that can facilitate more self-awareness and better thought patterns. I've met many payroll managers who feel stuck, frustrated, and unfulfilled. Going to work every day is mundane because they always feel like they're working with one hand tied behind their back. Nothing moves as efficiently as they would like; the root problems remain unresolved, and no one listens. In their anguish, they resign themselves to being powerless and incapable of changing anything. Some of these individuals aren't just smart, but extremely hard-working and highly skilled. Yet this is the fate they have to settle for? If that touches your heartstrings in any way, know that you are not alone. The reality of the matter is that nothing will change until you change. The real enemy of your life and the thief in the night coveting your dream lifestyle isn't someone at the organization. Life isn't against you. Suppression is not the modus operandi of life. That feeling of powerlessness and tendency to blame are not only unhealthy, but they also pull you deeper into the very experiences you despise. So, I will encourage you—just as I've done to hundreds of fellow payroll professionals—and urge you to stop looking to someone else to "fix" things. Instead, it is time for you to look within, recalibrate, rethink, and reassess your position. How strong is your mindset? Is it a fixed or growth mindset? Does your mind work for you or against your ambitions?

If you could learn how to develop a winner's mindset, how would that transform your career and lifestyle?

The Great Lie

Anyone who desires to play golf quickly discovers that it is challenging. Knowing what to do and actually doing what you know you should be doing are two different things, and it's often difficult to align the two in each swing. Keeping your thoughts and mental state in check for the entire play is no easy feat, and this is, in fact, the whole game of golf. After years of playing golf, I'm still a mere amateur, and while I've won several competitions (with a handicap of six at this point), the fact is, unless I put in the effort, my results will be less than amusing. I think that's a perfect mirror of how life works, wouldn't you agree?

Many factors are outside a golfer's control. The wind, the course conditions, and the ball's behavior after it's been hit are all-natural forces that no player can control. However, pro golfers don't waste their mental energy trying to control these factors. Instead, they focus on what they can control: their own swing, their mental state, and their strategy. When a pro golfer hits a bad shot, they don't dwell on it or let it impact their next shot. Instead, they stay focused on their strategy and adjust their mindset accordingly. They may take a deep breath, refocus their energy, and approach the next shot with a clear and confident mindset.

This ability to adjust and maintain a positive mindset is crucial in golf and all aspects of life. It's easy to become frustrated or discouraged when encountering setbacks or challenges. But what good will that do?

In global payroll, much like the game of golf, mastery lies in the delicate balance between knowledge and execution. Just as golfers learn that knowing the proper techniques is not enough, payroll professionals understand that bridging the gap between theory and practice is where true expertise emerges. Let me share a story that vividly illustrates this metaphor.

Imagine a golfer who meticulously studies the game's fundamentals, invests in top-of-the-line equipment, and envisions their shots with remarkable clarity. Yet, as they approach the tee, doubts and distractions creep into their minds. The pressure of the moment overwhelms them, and their swing falters, sending the ball astray. The gap between what they knew they should do and what they actually did widens, undermining their performance. Similarly, as a global payroll professional, you possess a wealth of technical knowledge, navigating the complexities of different countries, cultures, and regulations. You are adept at preparing meticulously, perfecting your techniques, and meeting deadlines. But even though you might be good at your job, there are too many factors out of your control, e.g., when HR doesn't send you accurate data on time. And all of a sudden, you're faced with a significant problem that could impact payroll for that month. In such instances, if you fail to apply your expertise and everything you've learned, or if your mental state is off, it will likely be a terrible month. You'll end up disappointing many people, including yourself. It wasn't your fault, but blaming forces out of your control doesn't help resolve anything. It only causes senior leadership to perceive you as incompetent, driving you further into that victim state.

Like the golfer who understands they cannot control external factors such as wind or course conditions, you face a dynamic landscape beyond your immediate influence. And, just as the golfer learns to focus on what they can control, you can empower yourself to do the same.

You can control your preparation, ensuring you communicate effectively with key stakeholders and create contingency plans that enable you to get what you need when you need it. You can maintain a resilient and optimistic mental state, even in the face of unexpected hurdles. You can refine your techniques and leverage the right tools to optimize your payroll operations. And most importantly, you can choose how to respond and adapt once you've taken the proverbial swing.

The lessons that golf has bestowed upon me as an avid amateur player resonate deeply with the challenges I encounter in life and business. Through golf, I've learned the invaluable lesson of focusing on what I can control—acknowledging that my preparation, mental fortitude, technical expertise, and adaptive responses hold the key to success. I've come to recognize that the more self-awareness I have, the easier it is to adjust my mindset and game whenever things don't go as planned. And trust me; things rarely go as planned, no matter how promising the weather seems. Mistakes happen often, but great golfers understand that failure is a natural part of the game, so they don't let setbacks affect their confidence or mental state.

A Fresh Start Each Month

In the world of payroll, you have the opportunity to hit reset every thirty days. This unique advantage allows you to recreate and improve your performance month after month, even if it's just by 10 percent. So, despite facing a complete disaster in last month's payroll, a new one is already on the horizon, providing you with a fresh chance to improve things. Of course, you still need to address and clean up any mistakes from the past, as neglecting them would be unwise. However, you can stop the bleeding and say, "I'm going to give my best effort to ensure this month's payroll is done accurately and on time."

Just like a golfer who sees each swing as an opportunity to enhance and reinvent their game, you have the chance to do things right each month. Instead of allowing last month's errors to spill over and create an ongoing mountain of problems, you can put an end to the cycle and implement a new approach that works better. Each month serves as a fresh canvas to improve and refine your payroll practices, making incremental progress and striving for excellence.

Now, of course, that's easier said than done, and perhaps you don't enjoy golf, or any sport for that matter. Could you still extract some valuable insight that boosts your transformation? Well, here's a good one. Think about what enables an excellent golfer to stay calm, confident, composed, and focused on hitting their next target in the face of adversity. The secret is their training and mental preparation. All great golfers spend countless hours practicing their swing, analyzing their technique, and studying the course. They know their strengths and weaknesses and have a game plan for approaching each hole. Additionally, they work day and night to cultivate a winner's mindset. In the words of Sun

Tzu, the battle is won before it's ever fought because the golfer invests time sharpening their mental and physical state.

A pro golfer relies on their training and mental focus during a play. They don't try to force a shot or change their technique to compensate for external factors. Instead, they trust their swing and execute it with precision and control. When you show up at the office, are you relying on your training, game plan, and mental focus? Or do you get thrown off by external factors and overcompensate in unproductive ways? You may not be a real athlete playing a sport, but you are meant to be the champion in your world. That means you should nurture your mind with the same care, discipline, and commitment that athletes deploy in their careers. So, this concept of cultivating a new mental state isn't a motivation strategy. It isn't about hype or giving you a quick rush of dopamine. You don't need to drown in affirmations and positive thinking. That's not what we're here to do. The intention is to learn the difference between a mental state that serves you and your ambition and one that pulls you down into despair and mediocrity.

A winner's mindset enables you to focus on what you can control. It teaches your brain how to start trusting more in your training and strategy, and it forces you to train and prepare more so that every obstacle becomes a stepping stone to greatness. A winner's mindset owns their role and responsibilities, no matter what. When you adopt this mindset, you will realize that regardless of the people around you causing these problems, you have the power to fix things and get things done. If you recognize and accept that it's your task to lead the organization through the changes necessary to get the department where it needs to be and that no one from other departments or senior leadership will come and do it for you, things start shifting for the better because you switch from always playing defense and feeling powerless to being proactive and in charge.

That's how you escape the life that has, until this point, brought you nothing but pain and disappointment. The more you elevate your training and mental preparation, the higher you will rise, and one day soon, you'll look back with wonder because your life will be shockingly different from what it used to be.

If you're starting to see what's waiting for you on the other side of your current mindset and are ready to take the plunge, we must add another crucial ingredient here: commitment.

Commitment

During the introduction, we discussed commitment as one of the four C's as essential ingredients for success. And yet, it's worth reiterating here because our society tends to undermine the importance of commitment in the pursuit of success, excellence, happiness, and all things good. The C word is like a tough pill to swallow, so most so-called gurus and motivators prefer to gloss over it. Many would rather do anything else than pay the real price to get what they desire, and that's why industries like weight loss still exist. Like other tough life skills, commitment isn't something many enjoy. It's easy to nod and agree with me when things are easy and comfortable, but once life happens and it gets uncomfortable, most pull back. Unfortunately, the path ahead requires commitment; otherwise, you'll never escape the current reality. Commitment is what enables us to navigate unpleasant change. It keeps us on the straight and narrow, focused on the end goal, until the storm clears out and we emerge victorious.

Commitment isn't about depriving yourself of something. It's about making yourself a promise that you'll stay the course until you achieve your chosen goal. So it's not hard or painful. The pain, struggle, and suffering come from the habits, thought patterns, and beliefs that challenge the realization of the goal. In other words, it's the part of you that prefers to stay in the safety of your comfort zone that fights with you and causes that unpleasant experience when you've committed to transforming something in your life.

The people who struggle with commitment the most are usually afraid of failure or lack confidence in their abilities. Truth be told, committing to something is scary because it feels risky. Our brains don't like exposure to physical, emotional, or financial failure, so instead, we naturally retreat and abandon the goal once things get heated. The crazy part is that sometimes (most of the time), that perceived risk is just that perceived. It's the brain's attempt at self-preservation and protection. So, the risk is internal and entirely made up of everything except hard facts. I've also noticed that people who struggle with commitment tend to get overwhelmed, overworked, and overburdened with responsibilities. There's an inability to prioritize, which leads to poor focus and performance. For that reason, we talked about purpose in Chapter Three of this book because learning to think differently and be intentional with your actions is the only way to overcome some obstacles.

If you want your ambitions to become more than wishful thinking, if you genuinely want to be excellent in your field and receive the respect, admiration, and reward that comes with a successful career, commitment is key. And with that comes the need to go all in and bet on yourself. The issue at hand isn't to take reckless risks like a gambler in Las Vegas hoping to take the house down (the house can never be taken down). I'm giving you the invitation and opportunity to recognize that you need to bet everything on yourself. That doesn't mean mindlessly and impulsively jumping in. Instead, we want to help you develop a strong sense of commitment that is strategic and rooted in your core values and priorities.

Where commitment begins ...

Real commitment is rooted in your self-awareness and a deep understanding of who you are, what drives you, and what matters to you as an individual. Once you know that, you can align your personal goals with your organization's goals and, through your values, cultivate a sense of purpose and motivation that drives you all the way to the summit.

Reflection time: Core values ...

What are your core values? Write down your top three to five core values and notice what comes up for you.

Our core values are the guiding principles that shape our beliefs, attitudes, and behavior. These values help us make important decisions, set priorities, and determine what is most important. However, many people struggle to identify their core values. They may have a general sense of what they believe, but they may not have taken the time to articulate their values explicitly.

If reflecting on and naming your values feels confusing and challenging, here are two simple exercises to get you thinking in the right direction:

Exercise #1: Consider the experiences that have shaped your life. What stands out? What matters most to you? Think about the times in your life when you felt most alive, fulfilled, and proud. What were the circumstances that made you feel this way? What values were being expressed in those moments?

For example, if you felt most alive and fulfilled while volunteering at a homeless shelter, the value of compassion and service may be important to you.

Exercise #2: I invite you to imagine your ideal life for the next five minutes. What would it look like if you could design your life exactly the way you wanted it? What values would be expressed in that lifestyle?

For example, if you imagine a life full of adventure and exploration, the values of freedom and creativity may be important to you.

Beyond Values

Values are one of the ways we begin to reshape our relationship with commitment. But it goes beyond that. To live a committed life, we must also build a support system. That may include surrounding ourselves with like-minded individuals who share our goals and can provide encouragement and accountability. This is where a community of peers and mentors who can help us stay on track becomes essential.

Life is only becoming more complex and challenging. Our profession won't get easier as global trade increases, but we can get stronger. High performance in our industry isn't a lone wolf game because we operate in a space that relies heavily on collaboration, communication, and continued education. There are many moving parts to this payroll system, and the best among us realize that commitment also expresses itself in the form of a strong support structure that helps us stay on track and committed to our goals.

To meet that aim, we're connecting like-minded individuals in our talent community where they get to share, receive free resources from our team of experts, and learn the Payrollmind DNA and framework we've developed over the years. We encourage you to join our global community to connect with your peers and our team of payroll experts, so you can dive even deeper into the concepts shared in this book. If you know that developing a growth mindset is the next best step for your career and you're ready to commit to embracing challenges, shifting beliefs, and viewing setbacks as opportunities, we are here to support you.

Remember, you have the potential to build your career to greater heights, and rather than view failure as finality, you can build resilience and cultivate the determination and perseverance that will keep you committed even when things are tough. This is what our industry needs—more payroll specialists and leaders who understand that they have the power to impact change within an organization. It begins with recognizing that they can change and design a lifestyle and career that unlocks their fullest potential.

If you bet on yourself, that's one of the best risks you will ever take. Now, I'm going to assume you're still reading this because you've made that commitment. That means it's time to roll up your sleeves and work on leveling up the only thing you can control.

Focusing on What You Can Control

Success in any endeavor comes down to habits. Winning is a habit. Losing is a habit. The habits you create for yourself make or break your life and career. In payroll, developing the habit of focused activities where you tackle one major problem at a time in an environment that facilitates critical thinking, creativity, and productivity is necessary. I always encourage payroll professionals to identify the moments of the day for peak performance when they can give their best and dedicate such time to real work instead of meetings and unimportant tasks. That is one of the best ways to start seeing an internal and external shift.

At a fundamental level, when you're running payroll, you've got to gain clarity over your calendar and deadlines. Figure out beforehand what data you need and where that data should come from. Instead of continuing that victim mindset that often thinks, "Let's wait and see how HR screws me over this month," you need to take a more proactive approach—a winner's mindset that says, "Let me do XYZ to ensure HR doesn't screw me over this month as they did last." Feel the difference? That incremental improvement we discussed earlier is only possible when you make clear agreements with all relevant stakeholders. The people who can either make or break your ability to accomplish your tasks accurately and in a timely manner should respect, admiration, and reward that comes with a successful career, commitment is key. And with that comes the need to go all in and bet on yourself. The issue at hand isn't to take reckless risks like a gambler in Las Vegas hoping to take the house down (the house can never be taken down). I'm giving you the invitation and opportunity to recognize that you need to bet everything on yourself. That doesn't mean mindlessly and impulsively jumping in. Instead, we want to help you develop a strong sense of commitment that is strategic and rooted in your core values and priorities.

Where commitment begins ...

Real commitment is rooted in your self-awareness and a deep understanding of who you are, what drives you, and what matters to you as an individual. Once you know that, you can align your personal goals with your organization's goals and, through your values, cultivate a sense of purpose and motivation that drives you all the way to the summit.

Reflection time: Core values ...

What are your core values? Write down your top three to five core values and notice what comes up for you.

Our core values are the guiding principles that shape our beliefs, attitudes, and behavior. These values help us make important decisions, set priorities, and determine what is most important. However, many people struggle to identify their core values. They may have a general sense of what they believe, but they may not have taken the time to articulate their values explicitly.

be properly handled. Effective communication is the key to this, and we'll talk more about that in an upcoming chapter so you can learn different ways to approach the various personalities you'll need to align with to get things done.

Eliminate Distractions: They Poison Your Performance

Sometimes, distractions are completely justified. They come in the form of unnecessary meetings or more minor issues that are important but not high-priority or mission-critical. Anything that gets in the way of you running a successful payroll this month, no matter how factual and important, should be viewed as a distraction. The last tip I will share to help you get better with your payroll this month is to identify your points of leverage.

Sure, there are many recurring problems to resolve in your department, and granted, last month's payroll issues are still unresolved, but trying to fix everything at once will only leave you exhausted and incapable of doing a great job this month. As you compile your priorities for the new month, try to include only one old issue to resolve at a time. So, for example, if you realize you're having problems with new hires and ex-employees, don't attempt to fix both problems at once. Start by resolving the new hires' issue and ensuring the new people coming in are onboarded correctly. That way, you have resolved an issue that would continue to make your life impossible over the coming months. It also ensures that you have happier employees because new people are more likely to perform better if they have fewer issues.

The same approach should be used for employees who are exiting the company. Make sure to pay them correctly and streamline that process so that you get fewer complaints and a faster, more efficient employee exit strategy in the future. Just by adjusting and improving the new hires and those who are leaving (one at a time), you've already improved and resolved the two big extremes that usually create a lot of frustration for the payroll department. Once these two are aligned, you can start addressing everything in between.

Part 2

Chapter 05:
Effective Communication

Recognizing the impact of communication in your career is a hack that will serve your future ambitions well, regardless of the chosen field, because effective communication is the cornerstone of success in any business function. In global payroll, where diverse cultures, languages, differing time zones, and regulatory environments intersect, communicating clearly and authentically becomes even more critical. And if you're concerned about getting buy-in from senior leadership or other department heads to further your agenda, then this is the very skill you'll need to master because influence is impossible in the absence of clear, effective communication, so pay keen attention to the following pages.

There are three phases that are always in play when dealing with any relationship-building activity: forming, challenging, and elevating the relationship. Knowing how to integrate each of these components into all the various relationships you will need to manage as a global payroll professional could be the difference between a thriving career and a job you hate because you're surrounded by people you can't stand. My conviction is that communication is the crux. By communication, I don't mean becoming an aggressive loudmouth or someone who constantly disturbs or disrupts. Instead, I mean knowing who you are, speaking your truth mindfully and with the best intentions, and adopting your message to match the filters and paradigms of those you'd like to influence. It's about expressing yourself confidently and then circling back to your audience to ensure they heard your message the way you intended them to receive it so they can leave there with clarity and no misunderstanding.

It doesn't matter how excellent your technical skills are. Your work will always feel unbearable if we can't transform you into a better, more eloquent, and more mindful communicator. That's why I'm pouring my insights from firsthand experience and observation around what it means to be an effective communicator, why it matters, and how it could impact your success in payroll.

What's Your Communication Style, and Why That Matters

Anyone who has been around me, either socially or professionally, can attest to the fact that my communication style is very straightforward and bold, and some might even say pretty aggressive. I call it like I see it. I'm not a fan of complex, vague concepts, so I'm always looking to simplify even the most intricate subject matters for myself and the people around me. For some of my audiences, especially those from similar cultural backgrounds, my communication style is a breath of fresh air and a most welcomed voice in board rooms where too much diplomacy gets in the way of actual results. For others, however, my style of communication is extremely intimidating. That is especially true for cultures with different verbal and nonverbal communication styles. After decades of dealing with Chinese, Japanese, American, Italian, Spanish, French, and other nationalities, I've learned to include modifiers and other language techniques that help facilitate better communication between myself and my audience to minimize misunderstandings and amplify rapport.

Crunching numbers and processing payroll is part of the job description for a payroll professional, but that's not all you need to learn. Hard skills get you the techniques you need to do your job well. Soft skills like effective communication help you excel and achieve great things in the department and across the organization. It's often thought that people are the purview of HR because everyone thinks communicating with people is purely a human resources function. The truth is, global payroll is a people-facing job as well. You need buy-in from a lot of people to do your job well. The stakeholders that interface with you internally and externally will only do their part well if you know how to convey information in a manner that enables you to build trust, resolve issues, and ensure your agenda doesn't get tossed to the sidelines.

Effective communication is the holding glue that makes collaboration and teamwork possible. Building good communication skills, specifically as a global payroll manager, has profound short- and long-term benefits for your career, team, and organization. The better a communicator you become, the easier it will be to motivate your team to get more done with better results, fewer misunderstandings, and greater accuracy. And who doesn't love accurate, error-free results? When communication is efficient, straightforward, and fortified by clear KPIs, there's increased trust among team members and colleagues, greater productivity, and higher job satisfaction. On the other hand, poor communication often leads to misunderstandings, conflict, resentment, and costly mistakes.

The High Cost of Poor Communication

Extensive research unequivocally demonstrates the detrimental consequences of poor communication practices. As a discerning global payroll professional, it is crucial to recognize and address this critical aspect to ensure optimal outcomes for your organization. Numerous studies illustrate the far-reaching effects of ineffective communication. In fact, research conducted by the Project Management Institute illuminates that inadequate communication contributes to project failures in one-third of cases. These failures often result in costly delays, budget overruns, and disgruntled stakeholders. Organizations that struggle with communication deficiencies witness a decline in employee engagement, a dip in productivity levels, and an alarming rise in turnover rates. The Society for Human Resource Management further substantiates the significance of communication by highlighting its role as a primary cause of workplace conflicts and low employee morale. Within the context of payroll management, the repercussions of poor communication can be especially profound.

Misunderstandings and miscommunications regarding critical factors such as employee hours, benefits, or deductions can lead to inaccurate calculations and payment discrepancies. These errors affect individual employees and erode their trust in the payroll department and, ultimately, the organization.

As a global payroll professional, you bear the responsibility of mitigating these risks and fostering a culture of effective communication within your team and across the organization. Miscommunication is a growing issue across every department, but it's even more costly for us in payroll. David Grossman reported in "The Cost of Poor Communications" that a survey of 400 companies with 100,000 employees each cited an average loss per company of $62.4 million per year because of inadequate communication to and between employees.

Poor Communication Makes You Invisible and Ineffective

In the world of payroll, poor communication can result in late payments, inaccurate tax reporting, and payroll-related legal disputes. This places unnecessary financial strain on the organization and damages its reputation. Imagine a scenario where James, the payroll manager at a large tech company, receives incomplete or inaccurate information from Beatrice, head of HR. Their communication breakdown leads to incorrect calculations, delayed payments, and dissatisfied employees. This sort of thing is more common than we'd like to believe. At times, the miscommunication can be so far-reaching that it snowballs into inaccurate tax reporting or failure to comply with other legal requirements, resulting in hefty penalties and legal complications. As the strain among the colleagues grows, more and more team members get entangled in this web of poor communication until, soon enough, no one is telling anyone anything. People are overlooking errors even if they spot them because they are too afraid of the volcanic eruption it would create. Such a hostile and fragmented work environment is toxic for everyone in the department and often hinders career growth.

Meanwhile, the CEO and other C-suite executives at the top know nothing of these underlying issues. All they see are lazy, unreliable underperformers who never get the job done.

Why Finding Your Voice Matters

Managing complex payroll processes involving multiple countries, currencies, and compliance requirements with diverse individuals is no easy feat. In such a dynamic environment, accurate and transparent communication is key to avoiding misunderstandings, errors, and compliance breaches. Authentic communication is the only way to convey information, establish trust, foster relationships, and demonstrate respect for your colleagues.

But to communicate authentically, you need to find your voice and confidence. Your voice represents your unique perspective, insights, and values. These help shape your communication style. The more you can identify your communication style and develop that unique voice, the easier it will be for others to listen with receptivity and respect your authenticity and confidence. Finding your voice isn't about copying someone else or forcing yourself to communicate in a way that you believe might be better received by others. In fact, the worst thing you can do when developing communication skills is to force yourself to portray a communication style that you feel would be more socially appropriate.

Authentic communication is rooted in transparency and honesty. You must be forthright about challenges, changes, and potential pitfalls. Doing so builds credibility and strengthens stakeholder relationships across different cultures and time zones. This form of communication is crucial in preventing misunderstandings that could lead to legal issues or damaged professional relationships.

What Does Authentic Communication Look Like for a Payroll Professional?

01. **Transparency:** That means openly discussing challenges, uncertainties, and potential risks associated with your processes. It's about candidly admitting when certain information is unavailable or when there is a need for further investigation.
02. **Cultural Sensitivity:** One-size-fits-all communication does not apply in a global context. You must learn to respect and adapt to the diverse cultural backgrounds of your audience. For example, I'm aware that in the presence of my Asian clients and colleagues, I need to select my words and tone with greater caution to ensure things don't get misinterpreted the wrong way. You will also need to learn this skill so you can vary your communication while still maintaining authenticity.

You must learn to be more mindful of preferences for hierarchy and comfort levels with directness, knowing when to strike a balance between clarity and respect for cultural norms— going back to my Asian colleague's example. If I'm meeting with an Indian payroll manager and his CFO, there are specific answers I wouldn't get from him, especially if he assumes the CFO will not receive the news positively. I would need to meet him privately and probe for the answers I need in an environment where he's more comfortable. That is a subtle yet potent expression of hierarchical cultural norms in our global society, and yes, it absolutely impacts performance.

> 03. **Active Listening:** Active listening is a communication skill that involves hearing the words being spoken, fully engaging with the speaker, understanding their message, and demonstrating your attentiveness and interest. It's a way of focusing on the speaker's verbal and nonverbal cues to better understand their thoughts, feelings, and perspectives. It's one of the best ways to make someone feel heard and valued. And when you make others feel heard, they will reciprocate the same. You must learn to actively listen to your stakeholders' concerns, questions, and feedback. Active listening signals that their opinions are valued and considered, fostering a sense of belonging and encouraging further engagement.
> 04. **Clarity:** Precision in communication is pivotal. When complex payroll issues are explained in convoluted language or technical jargon, they can be compounded and become more complicated. To ensure understanding, use clear and concise language, avoiding

unnecessary complexity. Visual aids, such as flowcharts or infographics, can aid in conveying intricate processes when appropriate.

05. **Two-Way Communication:** Encourage open dialogue by posing open-ended questions and seeking input from various stakeholders. This approach fosters an environment where diverse viewpoints are appreciated, leading to innovative solutions that might not have been possible with a unilateral communication style.

06. **Commitment:** Communication alone won't help you drive your team forward and accomplish your targets unless it is paired with commitment. Each time I engage in communication with my team or clients, I never leave that session without confirming the "next steps" and what each one is accountable for before the next meeting. That helps me accomplish two things; first, I use that summary time to listen to what the other person took away from the conversation so that we avoid misinterpretations and misunderstandings about action steps. I also use that time to secure a verbal acknowledgment that acts as a commitment to me that the other person knows what to do and will get it done at an agreed- upon timeline.

Cultural Dexterity (Cultural Competence)

Cultural dexterity, or cultural competence, refers to effectively interacting and working with individuals from diverse cultural backgrounds. It is about understanding, respecting, and adapting to different cultural norms, values, beliefs, and communication styles. Cultural dexterity goes beyond simply acknowledging cultural differences; it requires the capacity to navigate and thrive in multicultural environments. That's something you must do in global payroll because you're constantly working with different people from different departments and cultural and educational backgrounds. The more you can improve your cultural competence, the easier it will be to build connections, influence decision-making with relevant stakeholders, and build bridges that overcome differences. In short, your ability to problem-solve and lead people to achieve a common goal will exponentially grow.

Cultural dexterity involves:

1. **Awareness:** Being aware of one's own cultural biases, assumptions, and limitations, as well as recognizing the diversity of others' perspectives.
2. **Knowledge:** Gaining knowledge about various cultural backgrounds, traditions, practices, and histories to better understand the context in which others operate.
3. **Adaptability:** Being able to modify your behavior, communication style, and approach to suit the preferences and norms of different cultural contexts.
4. **Empathy:** Cultivating empathy and understanding for the experiences and challenges individuals from diverse backgrounds face.
5. **Effective Communication:** Having the skills to communicate clearly and respectfully with individuals who may have different language skills or communication styles.

6. **Conflict Resolution:** Navigating and resolving conflicts that arise due to cultural misunderstandings or differences.
7. **Inclusivity:** Creating an inclusive environment where all individuals feel valued and can contribute their unique perspectives.
8. **Open-Mindedness:** Approaching interactions with curiosity, an open mind, and a willingness to learn from others' viewpoints.

Communicating with Stakeholders and Senior Leadership For Stronger Partnerships

Effective communication with stakeholders and senior leadership is essential for building stronger partnerships and ensuring alignment within an organization. There are always three components of relationship building at play: initiating or forming the relationship through nurturing techniques, challenging it for continued growth, and ultimately elevating it so you don't become complacent just because things are going well. These three apply to any and all stakeholder relations.

In your position, stakeholders fall into various categories, including internal team members working in other departments, senior leadership, employees who depend on you to deliver payroll, external stakeholders like suppliers, and many more. Your role deals with many moving parts, each with a unique group of people who help you do your best work.

Becoming proactive with how you approach, nurture, grow, and maintain all the key relationships is a wise move because, in the long run, it ensures you get to keep and execute your priorities, get better buy-in for your ideas, implement solutions more effectivity, and overall optimize how payroll runs within the organization. The key thing is to recognize that you can't approach, address, or communicate with everyone precisely the same way. When speaking to your team members, the CFO, CEO, or a supplier, you need to meet them at their level and use language they can resonate with. For example, when speaking with a payroll team member, you can use internal jargon and fuss over the nitty-gritty of the process, but when meeting with the C-suite executives, you'll need to tweak your approach to have as little jargon as possible and to carry a more holistic point of view that ties directly to the growth and longevity of the company. Many global payroll leaders struggle to make this shift because they assume they must pretend to be something they aren't. That couldn't be further from the truth. You need to know your role, agenda, problems, and solutions well enough that you can plug them into the overall agenda and goals of the organization. Makes sense?

Evoking curiosity and interest from relevant parties:

The reality of the matter is that very few people in your organization have the headspace or interest to understand your needs, priorities, or processes in payroll. Most leaders and heads of departments only think about payroll when there's a problem. That is neither good nor bad. It's upon you to take ownership of your role and to find creative, mutually beneficial ways to raise interest and curiosity. The more internal stakeholders can see the value of engaging in payroll-related talks, the likelier it will be to see more of your agenda being addressed when it matters. The level of maturity of the payroll function within your company, as well as the curiosity of members in other departments, impacts your process and how easy it is to resolve some of the major problems we all face when trying to run payroll. And it's up to you to do your homework to uncover some of these hidden gems so you can get clarity on the real situation. Do you need to promote more knowledge sharing with relevant parties? Are you going to need to be more proactive in raising issues that directly impact payroll and overall business objectives that others might be missing?

These are a few of the many questions you need to ask yourself. Most of the time, the biggest step to take is communicating with relevant parties and doing it intentionally and genuinely. I have lost count over the years of the number of times when I've sat across meetings that were getting nowhere because people simply couldn't see eye-to-eye. However, when I investigated deeper into the matter, I realized that the lack of progress was rooted in poor communication. Most notable was my recent experience with a fairly mature company. As I sat in the room with its senior leaders and facilitated an open dialogue to tackle their problems strategically, some of the reactions puzzled me. At some point, I had to ask, "Guys, how often do you have conversations like these?" To my surprise, they confessed that beyond the weekly emails, they couldn't recall ever sitting down in a single meeting with all heads of departments to actively problem-solve, which meant their company's communication strategy was clearly broken. And when communication breaks down, it's only a matter of time before the bottom line suffers, even for a growth company.

Dealing with senior leadership requires a holistic, problem-solving approach and plenty of communication:

One key learning I'd like you to take from this section on communicating with senior leadership is this. Your mindset and communication need to mature and evolve so you can stop trying to put band-aids on things or wait for solutions to come from the top. Every leader wants to know that the global payroll professional brings something to the table that will move the business forward.

So your job isn't just to seek solutions that solve your department's next thirty-day cycle, but to uncover and create solutions that positively impact your entire organization. This way, the better you'll become at assessing and diagnosing complex business issues and synthesizing solutions that help decision-makers say yes to your agenda.

When engaging with senior leaders and executives, it's important to follow some fundamental rules to maximize the impact of your interactions.

First and foremost, avoid band-aid solutions. Take ownership of problems as they arise and fight to get to the root of the issue so it can be resolved once and for all. And when you bring your problems, always come up with potential solutions that can be discussed and debated. During heated discussions, refrain from going on the defense and trying to play the victim, especially when dealing with senior leadership. This is especially important when you know you're not at fault. Acknowledge their concerns and questions with openness and a willingness to address issues constructively. Defensiveness can hinder productive dialogue and erode trust, which is crucial for a strong partnership.

Another crucial point to remember is not to overwhelm leadership with minutiae or day-to- day details. Senior leaders are typically focused on the bigger picture and strategic goals.

Provide them with concise, high-level information highlighting key points and impacts without delving into unnecessary specifics.

To instill confidence in your capabilities, display unwavering self-assurance during your interactions with senior leadership. Confidence reflects your competence and reassures them that you can handle challenges effectively. It's a trait that inspires trust and respect.

When engaging in conversations with leaders, aim to "execute rainmaking" discussions. This means speaking to them at their level of understanding and in a language that resonates with their strategic perspective. Tailor your communication to address their concerns and objectives directly, demonstrating your ability to contribute to their overarching goals.

Furthermore, it's essential to maintain a broader horizon during discussions with leadership. Think long term and align your ideas and proposals with the organization's future vision. By showing that you're focused on the organization's sustained success, you demonstrate your commitment to its growth and prosperity.

Lastly, exercise business acumen when communicating with senior leaders. Understand their objectives and priorities, and provide insights into how your initiatives or ideas align with these goals. By clearly demonstrating what they want to achieve and identifying the next best steps, you position yourself as a valuable contributor to the organization's success.

Self-Confidence and Effective Communication

Confidence plays a vital role in effective communication. When you believe in your abilities and have confidence in your message, you can deliver it with conviction and influence others. That self-belief and conviction in your message make you authentic and worth following. The more authentic you are when dealing with others, the greater your level of credibility and influence with colleagues, senior leaders, and employees.

It creates an environment where open and honest communication can flourish. You can only embrace authenticity as part of your communication style if you learn to embrace your individuality, strengths, and the things that make you great at your job. Allow those to shine unapologetically.

If there's a problem, don't sweep it under the rug. Deal with it head-on and ensure no lingering resentment is allowed within your team. Be an example for others. Demonstrate that effective communication isn't necessarily the loud, aggressive leader or the smooth talker.

Even the quiet and reserved can be powerful in their communication, as long as they express their values and principles through their words and actions. So, learn to speak from a position of authenticity and confidence because a healthy dose of high self-esteem is contagious, inspiring trust and respect from those around you.

How to Be Heard

If you want to be heard, there are two qualities you need. First, you must train yourself to be clear and precise when conveying information.

The payroll process involves intricate details, calculations, and compliance requirements. Get into the habit of breaking things down into simpler, easy-to-digest, and actionable points.

That will ensure the information is accurately understood and minimize the risk of errors or misunderstandings.

Have you ever engaged someone in a conversation and regretted that decision moments later when you got half-baked answers and mumbled words? If yes, then you know exactly what not to do!

Henceforth, your aim is to make an effort to simplify complex concepts, use plain language, and avoid technical jargon terms that may confuse others. Remember, most of your communication involves people who barely understand payroll. Leave the geeky jargon terms to your payroll group chats and use them when the information is made strictly for internal use or official legal affairs. The rest of the world just needs you to organize your thoughts before communicating and presenting information in a logical, structured, easy-to-grasp language.

The second quality you must develop if you want to be heard is the ability to be a great listener. Effective communicators don't just speak; they listen. Listen twice as much as you talk. That's the only way to fully understand the people around you. The more you can perceive their words, the meaning behind spoken words, and the nonverbal cues often communicated during interactions, the easier it becomes to convey responses that will resonate. Communication requires verbal and nonverbal understanding. It demands resonance between the parties involved. The more you learn to create resonance with others, the easier it will be for you to be heard. Over the years, I've realized that the more I worked on improving my listening skills, reading nonverbal communication, and embracing my individuality, the stronger and more effective my communication became.

Many of the best communicators I know also recommend continuous study and improvement of oneself to improve overall communication with others. So, pay attention to your current communication style. What's your usual tone, pace, and body language when dealing with others? How much jargon do you use when speaking with employees, senior leaders, and colleagues in different departments? How often do people give you that puzzled look as you answer their questions? Do you feel strong resistance to improving this aspect of your professional career? If so, find out why.

Emotional Intelligence and Empathy

To truly thrive, you must harness the power of emotional intelligence and empathy. Empathy is a key component of emotional intelligence, which involves recognizing and managing emotions in oneself and others. These invaluable traits enable you to navigate diverse cultures, build strong relationships, and effectively communicate across borders.

Emotional intelligence encompasses a range of abilities, including self-awareness, self- regulation, empathy, and social skills. As a global payroll manager, developing your emotional intelligence enables you to understand and manage your own emotions while effectively navigating the feelings of others.

1. **Self-Awareness**: Begin by cultivating self-awareness, which involves recognizing and understanding your own emotions, strengths, and limitations. Regular self-reflection, seeking feedback, and embracing personal growth opportunities will deepen your understanding of how your feelings impact your decision-making and interactions with others.
2. **Self-Regulation**: Building upon self-awareness, self-regulation involves constructively managing your emotions and behaviors. Practice techniques such as deep breathing, mindfulness, and stress management to maintain composure and make rational decisions, even in high-pressure situations.
3. **Empathy**: Empathy is the ability to understand and share the feelings of others. It plays a pivotal role in building strong relationships and fostering collabo-

ration. Empathy allows you to effectively tailor your communication style and approach to connect with individuals from diverse backgrounds and cultures. Actively listen to your colleagues, seek to understand their perspectives, and demonstrate genuine care and concern for their well-being.

The more you develop your emotional intelligence, the easier it will be to practice active listening. It's easier to give your fullest attention and demonstrate a genuine interest in another when your emotions are in check. You also get better at perspective-taking through the practice of empathy. And that increases your compassion and humanity. Sometimes, when dealing with a challenging circumstance, people just want to know that you've heard them and that you're human enough to want to support and assist them in resolving their issues. It takes empathy and emotional intelligence to successfully remove irrational emotions from your communication yet still appear approachable, professional, caring, and supportive.

Some of these concepts might feel unnatural or hard at first, but with practice and intent, they get better. How do you know your communication is improving? Take notice of how you deal with challenging conversations.

Navigating Difficult Conversations through Effective Communication

Taking emotion out of communication means approaching conversations and interactions rationally and objectively without allowing personal feelings to take over. It's like staying cool when the temperature around you heats up. Increased emotional intelligence will make diffusing hot topics and heated emotions a little easier. For example, I once worked with a company where the person in charge of payroll (let's call her Nancy) felt like the HR department, led by Judy, was causing her a lot of trouble. Nancy never talked to Judy about it. For months, she sat there in brooding resentment and tried to reciprocate the harsh treatment she received.

When I was brought in to help and listened to Nancy's side of the story, I realized she had done everything but confront the issue head-on. So I insisted we walk over to HR for a face- to-face with Judy. Nancy was very apprehensive, but I persisted and finally got the three of us in an office. I locked the door and asked the ladies to air out every single issue they had with one another. I stayed emotionally neutral and unattached to the arguments and heated discussions that raged on for over an hour. It took longer than I originally anticipated, but within a few hours, the battle was over, and these two ladies had finally overcome the months of assumptions, bitterness, and resentment that had piled on.

After that day, things started operating with greater efficiency, and we were able to improve overall payroll performance.

Given the fact that we know dealing with problems and sensitive issues is part of the job description as a global payroll professional, I suggest you take control of your emotions.

Here's why:

1. **Objective Decision-Making**: Emotions can cloud judgment and hinder rational decision-making. In the payroll department, decisions often involve sensitive matters such as compensation, benefits, or compliance issues. And we all know how emotional the topic of money can be. By removing emotions from the equation, you can make objective decisions based on facts, data, and established policies. That ensures fairness, consistency, and compliance with regulations.
2. **Maintaining Professionalism**: Payroll professionals serve as the face of the department and represent the entire organization. A calm and poised demeanor demonstrates the ability to handle complex issues with professionalism and integrity. Engaging in emotional communication can undermine professionalism and create a negative perception.
3. **Resolving Conflicts**: Conflicts can arise in any workplace, and the payroll department is no exception. When conflicts occur, it is essential to approach them with a level-headed and objective mindset. Emotionally charged communication can escalate conflicts and hinder productive resolutions. By removing emotions from the conversation, you can focus on understanding

the underlying issues, facilitating open dialogue, and finding mutually beneficial solutions.
4. **Building Trust and Credibility**: Effective communication builds trust and credibility with colleagues, employees, and executive leaders. Emotionally driven communication can erode trust and create barriers to collaboration. By taking the emotion out of communication, you'll foster an environment of trust where everyone feels heard, respected, and valued.
5. **Enhancing Collaboration:** The payroll department interacts with various departments, including HR, finance, and operations. Effective collaboration requires clear and concise communication focusing on facts and objectives rather than personal emotions. The more you take feelings out of the equation, the easier it becomes to focus on what matters. That leads to better collaborations and streamlined processes and gives you a cohesive and efficient payroll function that supports your ambitions and the organization's overall goals.

Developing the emotional intelligence and courage to have these tough conversations and let go of issues is a gift to yourself because tough conversations and disagreements are inevitable. You must learn that delicate dance between empathy and oversensitivity. One makes you a better communicator, and the other cripples your team.

At times, the uncomfortable conversations are with team members; other times, they involve an unhappy employee. Other times still, they involve senior leadership. So, how will you train your brand to remain unemotional and poised? That response won't kick in unless you've been practicing beforehand.

Reflection Time

If you're ready to commit to your career growth and transformation, here are three simple areas to apply effective communication and emotional intelligence to your role once you've laid a strong foundation.

#1: **Cross-Cultural Communication**: Interact with individuals from diverse cultures, adapting your communication for clarity. Consider language barriers, nonverbal cues, time zones, and cultural sensitivities.

#2: **Conflict Resolution**: Use emotional intelligence to navigate conflicts. Seek common ground, listen actively, and foster open dialogue. Demonstrate empathy to reach resolutions that maintain positive relationships.

#3: **Building Trust and Collaboration**: Demonstrate empathy and emotional intelligence to build trust. Understand colleagues' needs, promote open communication, and encourage collaboration—value diverse perspectives for a unified global payroll management team.

#4: **Commitment and KPIs**: Always end any session by circling back to your audience to ensure they heard and understood your intended message. Give clear KPIs that the intended audience can commit to and use their verbal acknowledgment to make the agreement on the next action steps and timelines.

To become the best and most effective communicator you can be, the rules of the game are very simple. And what matters most isn't that you change yourself to be socially acceptable. Instead, it's about increasing your awareness of who you are and your communication style so you can be more mindful when interacting with and building rapport with stakeholders. Authentic communication isn't about pretending to be something you're not. It's about being more of yourself and learning to adapt and tweak your message (not your personality) to better resonate with your intended audience. Once you have a better grasp on how you express yourself, it's time to roll up your sleeves and start solving problems … after all, that's the real job of global payroll.

Chapter 06:
Problem-Solving

As a payroll professional, the essence of being a true problem solver cannot be overstated. In board meetings, podcasts, and workshops, I've consistently underscored this fundamental truth: to excel in our field, one must be enthusiastic about diving headfirst into the intricate complexities that define global payroll. It's not merely about crunching numbers or processing transactions; it's about unraveling the intricacies of international tax laws, navigating cultural differences, and addressing the unique challenges that arise when managing payroll on a global scale. This chapter of this book is perhaps my favorite because it focuses on the profound importance of problem-solving skills. It serves as a validation for those who have always felt the innate connection between their passion for payroll and their innate problem-solving abilities. If you find yourself genuinely excited by the prospect of tackling payroll challenges that span borders, regulations, and cultures, then this is precisely where you belong, and the content of this resource is your compass for charting a successful career in our industry.

The skill of problem-solving is not an innate gift; it is a learnable and trainable ability that sets the stage for greatness. Whether you dream of becoming a C-suite executive or building a high-performing team recognized and respected throughout your organization, this is the muscle you want to exercise most. At my firm, the fundamental basis of the work we do with our pool of talented candidates, as well as the training we provide to the payroll teams we work with within organizations, is all with the intention of teaching payroll professionals to become self-sufficient problem solvers and holistic thinkers. Problem-solving in payroll is the difference between mediocrity and excellence. Throughout the pages that follow, I have distilled years of experience, insights, and hard-won knowledge to create a resource that will empower you as a global payroll professional. Consider this the culmination of my journey. I hope you derive as much enjoyment from reading it as I did in crafting it for you.

Transforming Challenges into Opportunities

At the heart of this mastery lie two enigmatic skill sets. The first is the analytical acumen that empowers individuals to transform and break down complexity into basic fundamentals that are easier to resolve. The second is creative thinking, which enables the same individuals to come up with "out of the box" intelligent solutions.

Perceptual alchemy and creative thinking allow payroll professionals to peer beyond the surface to delve into the essence of challenges. They employ these skills to dissect vast datasets, intricately woven payroll processes, and multifaceted relations that often create tension and friction in the payroll process. While the average payroll professional might stick to putting band-aids on problems, a true payroll professional will research, inquire, scrutinize, and investigate the root cause of issues—never backing down until he or she uncovers the discrepancies and subtle nuances that cause breakage in the payroll process and team collaboration. It takes both an analytical and creative mind to approach the payroll function this way. But even beyond analytical thinking, it takes a dedicated, courageous, and effective communicator to identify and address the underlying factors that fuel payroll inefficiencies. They are not constrained by the comfortable confines of established norms but harbor an audacious spirit to reimagine solutions. Their creative brilliance navigates the uncharted territories of global payroll management, where unconventional approaches may hold the keys to overcoming modern-day challenges.

The Mark of Self-Sufficiency and Independent Thinking

The true mark of an independent employee and a valuable asset to an organization doesn't come from a fancy resume. It's about demonstrating your self-sufficiency and ability to think logically, identify the root problems, creatively brainstorm potential solutions, make a decision about what you need to do next to create sustainable solutions, and take ownership and action in the direction of your solutions. Even after the resolution, you will still need time to reflect on what worked and what didn't, what mistakes were made, and what lessons can be derived from the experience to ensure a change in behavior based on the new information. All this is what actual problem-solving demands from us when we face a new challenge. Working independently and taking ownership of everything that gets in the way of running payroll makes you a self-sufficient problem solver. That doesn't mean you're a lone wolf. Great problem solvers know how to work independently as well as collaborate with others. They also know how to be resourceful even when resources are limited.

So the next time you're faced with a challenge and feel limited in some way, give yourself permission to take a step back, zoom out, and think holistically about the obstacle standing in your way. See it as a stepping stone to a greater version of yourself, and use the problem-solving framework introduced in this chapter so you can innovate new solutions and rise within your department as an independent thinker and a self-sufficient employee. That is one of the best ways to receive the recognition you deserve.

The Nature of the Beast

Global payroll is definitely not for everyone, but anyone willing to put in the work who has thick skin and the capacity to mature into critical soft skills like problem- solving can undoubtedly thrive. What matters isn't that you always do your job right, but that you can stay calm, focused, and amicable when things go wrong. Imagine for a moment you're caught up in a situation that causes payroll to be delayed, and you need to go report to your CFO or CEO that because of an unexpected issue, payroll won't be happening on time this month, which means employees aren't getting paid. Unhappy employees don't make for productive workers, so obviously, senior leadership will be infuriated by this news. You'll be on the receiving end of that frustration as people share their emotions and disappointments with you. In truth, you might have done 99% of the job right, but that 1% (which may not even be your fault) could be the culprit. Yet the spotlight on you is anything but favorable.

People rarely remember payroll leaders when things are going well but have no trouble highlighting their inefficiencies when something goes wrong. None of us go into payroll for the fame or recognition, and yet, it would be great if your seniors would periodically acknowledge the many months of smooth payroll. But if you only live for the praise, then the yelling and reprimanding that comes with delayed payroll will undoubtedly kill you.

Beyond analytical prowess and innovation, the hidden gem of becoming a powerful problem solver is that it forces you to approach the payroll function holistically. Rather than settling for short-term solutions that only solve for a single unit, extraordinary payroll professionals explore diverse angles, consider alternate viewpoints, and discern potential implications that may elude the uninitiated. They are concerned about meeting deadlines, serving their client on time, and how their actions impact the forward momentum of the entire organization.

At my consulting firm, where we work with both talent and large organizations, we always emphasize developing problem-solving and critical-thinking skills. We train payroll professionals to focus on root-cause issues and think about the different business units and how our solutions will benefit everyone, not just the payroll function. Shifting to this point of view isn't always easy and certainly doesn't happen by default. Over time, one learns to stack together specific skills that help strengthen that problem-solving muscle.

When running global payroll, the last thing you want is to be a bull charging forward and creating messes along the way (that's what a lack of critical thinking will do for you). Instead, you want to be the kind of global payroll professional who can identify root problems, develop sustainable solutions, and meticulously evaluate the associated risks. That way, you can raise red flags to senior leadership long before things escalate. So, how do you take your problem- solving skills to the next level?

The Sustainable Problem-Solving Process

My team and I have developed a framework we typically use when working with organizations and their payroll team. We broke it down into diagnosing, conceptualizing, aligning with business goals, implementing, and measuring results. Ideally, you want to approach problem-solving by first learning to effectively diagnose the root issues that stand in the way of you doing your best job. Once you've assessed and found the problem, be relentless about developing solutions that are not only sustainable long term but also align with your organization's values, objectives, and vision. Doing so ensures you can easily get buy in from senior leadership because a solution without support cannot go very far. Once you've demonstrated that you've got something that will benefit all stakeholders involved, follow through with implementation and track the effort to prove that your concept works. Of course, this simple framework only works because we continue to emphasize the importance of getting to know yourself as an individual first and foremost. The more grounded you are in yourself, the easier it is to apply frameworks and information. A strong problem solver isn't just analytical, creative, and a good communicator; they also know who they are and use that as a basis to build upon and execute their plans. So, while it might seem like all you need to do now is learn this problem-solving framework, my biggest advice to you, dear reader, is to invest as much time, energy, and resources as possible to know who you are. Then, be who you are so you can become who you need to be. That is the key to unlocking success with the frameworks we teach at my firm.

Evolving Excellence and Problem-Solving Skills

Anyone working in global payroll, assuming they don't hate their job, is already a problem solver; otherwise, they would quit. So it's not a question of whether you can be a problem solver ... you are. But how developed are your problem-solving and critical-thinking skills? To the degree that your skills are underdeveloped and operating below average, your performance and career suffer. Here are some quick questions to jolt your awareness of how strong you are as a problem solver:

1. How strong are you at recognizing patterns, discrepancies, and anomalies that elude others?
2. Are you a band-aid type of person, or do you prefer to delve deep into the root causes of problems?
3. Do you often find yourself thinking outside the box?
4. How good are you at seeking different perspectives, new angles, and potential implications before deciding?
5. Do you typically go for a risk-aware approach, weighing potential benefits against the risks and evaluating the drawbacks of each course of action?
6. Are you impulsive in your decision-making, or do you make informed choices as a result of a meticulous evaluation process?

Your genuine responses to those questions will already tell you plenty about your current problem-solving and critical-thinking levels. The intention is to nurture and groom these skills so you can continue to improve as a person and a professional.

An Ethical Imperative

Critical thinking and problem-solving in global payroll management are bound by a sacred covenant with ethics and legality. Extraordinary individuals hold themselves to the highest ethical standards, recognizing that their decisions impact the organization and the livelihoods and well-being of employees. If you found yourself in a dilemma regarding the classification of employee benefits for tax purposes, how would you approach this? Would you try to find a shortcut that minimizes tax liabilities but skirts the boundaries of legality? Or would you refuse to compromise and engage in exhaustive research, seeking legal counsel, and upholding the principles of transparency and legality? The actions you take in such situations speak volumes about who you are and what kind of professional you will become. Beyond personal character, it also endangers or preserves the organization's integrity, safeguarding the interests of employees. Ethical standards are often not discussed, but we cannot promote sustainable problem-solving as a skill and not underline this character trait.

Don't Avoid the Facts

Avoidance is poison fruit to a good problem solver, and the only antidote to grant you immunity now and in the future is to further develop your courage. You cannot get very far if all you do is avoid the issues that always appear when running global payroll. Dealing with people across different time zones, from different cultural backgrounds, with varying expectations and personal agendas means problems will always crop up, and it is your duty to face and handle the facts as presented to you. The sooner you do, the easier it will be to dismantle many of these issues. The trick I've used over the years that works wonders for me is that I do my best to prepare and plan for as much as I can, bearing in mind that the unexpected is bound to happen. And as long as a part of my brain anticipates the unexpected when it does show up, I don't go into panic mode. I simply acknowledge the unpleasant situation as falling under the category of the unexpected and move immediately to deploy my resources so we can come to a quick resolution. I can proactively jump into the unexpected because

I invest time in planning and prepping for the "knowns" so that I can have the bandwidth to tackle the "unknowns." For instance, if you know this month you're going to pay bonuses, then this is worth preparing for in advance because should something go wrong and the unexpected happens, you may end up missing that deadline, which will lead to overwhelm and frustration on your end—not to mention the migraine that you'll get from all the scrutiny and complaints of both your superiors and customer. Things will rarely go as perfectly as you want. And if you cannot deal with that and build infrastructure around you that enables you to deal with things going wrong, then cutting it as a global payroll professional will be tough.

This book is meant to get you thinking in the same way because, whether you realize it or not, the most productive payroll leader you look up to isn't effective because they know it all. They are also not perfect or flawless. Instead, they are better prepared and think differently than you. Imagine how much better your life would be if you could start operating at that same level.

Strategies to Increase Your Level of Problem-Solving

We've already acknowledged that problem-solving is about combining analytical, critical, and creative thinking and that you need to get better at facing the problem so you can resolve it rather than stick a band-aid on it. But before you can solve a problem, you need to know the root problem. So, one way of ensuring you're developing this skill is to self-observe as you move through obstacles. Take notice of how easy it is for you to go beyond surface-level issues and identify the core problems that would resolve the surface symptoms. Most people get stuck on surface issues. You want to practice the art of knowing the root cause and bringing it to stakeholders' awareness. Let them know what problems are worthy of attention and agree to disagree. Disagreeing with stakeholders about what the real problem is can be just as beneficial because it allows you to determine whether you need extra expert help from an objective third party or positions you to have clarity on what the organization genuinely cares about. Once the real problem is on the table, set out to create a plan that you and the team can execute. If your concern is the resources required to fix the problem, this is where resourcefulness comes into play. Be persistent in making a business case for yourself and win sponsorship from stakeholders so you can invest in the sustainable solution that will help drive the organization forward. If, for example, you're running a payroll of ten thousand with a team of four in your department, there will be limitations because your team won't have the capacity to fix the issue. But that shouldn't stop you. Suppose the plan is solid, and you know how to win partners because you've cultivated a Payrollmind DNA that enables you to persuade and positively influence stakeholders. In that case, you will receive the support you need to execute your plan.

Technology, Automation, and Problem-Solving

When I was a young man forging my career in payroll, I would prepare a paper document and send it over to the payroll vendor, who would, in turn, send over paper payslips, and I had to manually check that both my records and the payslips were a perfect match. It was a very taxing and manual job. Each payslip needed to be checked line by line, which quite frankly left plenty of room for human error. Today, everything is software, and we don't need human intervention for the check because artificial intelligence can take care of all that manual work in seconds with practically zero errors. While I am a huge advocate for technology and introducing systems for automation that are AI-led, my only concern is that we, as payroll professionals, don't create complexities and undue problems by misusing the tools in our possession. Just as a Tesla owner would never attempt to drive it across the river or off-road, to a similar extent, we learn the tools we use and utilize them only for the job they were designed to perform. That is, in fact, the best way to get the maximum benefits out of the tools and technological software that we're bringing into the payroll function.

To be clear, I do not suggest you avoid using technology and automation—quite the contrary. You must leverage automation and build systems for your payroll process that help streamline your work and increase efficiency. But do so intentionally so that you can get the best results. That begins with your source data. The more handoffs your data has, the higher the chances of corrupting it. Your system will only be as efficient as this first step, which should always be of primary concern to you; otherwise, the rest of the process breaks. If, however, you establish the right tools and collect clean data, then work with systems of automation that best help you reach your objectives. Artificial intelligence and robotics are relatively new, and we have years of work ahead of us before we can make them operate at the highest levels. They are also pretty costly, especially if you want complex solutions for a complex payroll function within a large organization. So don't feel pressured to go after the shinest or newest solutions.

Educate yourself on the various options available and choose the one that will do the best job at the price point that best suits your budget.

Problem-solving isn't just about making sure you hit the deadline for payroll on time in the next thirty days; it's also about taking ownership of the process, the technology, and the systems at play. Think about this for a moment. HR enters data into their system for the newest hire, and it goes without saying that payroll immediately needs this data to reflect on their payroll vendor system in order for this new employee to receive their first month's wage at the end of the thirty days, right? Who do you think would be the ideal person to take ownership of how this information will flow from HR to the payroll vendor? This is an ongoing debate and a question I'm always posing in board rooms. Unfortunately, it's tough to agree unanimously that ownership should belong to the payroll leader. Why? Because many believe it should be the responsibility of both HR and payroll. Here's my observation: When two chefs run the kitchen, nothing excellent gets served. That's why every Michelin-star restaurant only hosts one great chef at a time.

It's crucial that we have one leader taking charge at any given time. I have found the best way to control the payroll process and avoid being overwhelmed and disappointed is to take ownership of how the data moves from HR to payroll vendor. I believe that whichever role stands to lose the most in the event of delayed or corrupt data should be the one to take ownership of the process. And that means the payroll manager. When you learn to stop thinking like most payroll professionals and start thinking like the few great payroll leaders, you will experience more peace of mind and better results in your department. The idea of taking ownership makes problem-solving a lot more enjoyable and practical because, in essence, you can only resolve a problem when you decide to take responsibility for it. If you're still playing finger-pointing with employee data, you haven't fully taken responsibility, which means you cannot have the confidence you need to trust that your payroll function will run smoothly. So, the message here is pretty simple. Do you want a little more peace of mind back in your life? Would you like to level up your problem-solving skills? Take ownership of employee data from source to payroll vendor. That is one of the primary mental shifts you'll have to make. You must take full ownership of the source data you need to do your job so you can control how it's gathered, track its movement, and secure its validity without falling into the mercy of HR and other departments. Yes, that means doing more than your job description requires and working with people you may not particularly like, but that's what the next chapter is about. You're about to learn how to make the idea of ownership and problem-solving practical so you can finally start to operate like the top performers in global payroll. Are you ready?

Chapter 07:
Growing Partnerships

I once read a Kobe Bryant Facebook post where he stated the responsibility of being a leader and his views. "Sometimes, you must prioritize the success of the team ahead of how your own image is perceived ... I'd rather be perceived as a winner than a good teammate. I wish they both went hand in hand all the time, but that's just not reality," wrote Kobe. There's plenty that's right with this statement. While he may have gotten a lot of hate (most winners do), I'm not advocating for you to turn into a jerk, locking horns with every department head like a wild bull to get results. We must address the truth about what it takes to work with others to accomplish a mission.

Here's a question worth reflecting upon. Do you have to like everyone you work with to have a productive relationship? Better still, do you need to be appreciated by everyone for you to work well with others? It may seem silly, but most people are miserable in the workplace because they just don't know how to work productively with others.

The younger generation is especially struggling with this. In an era where positive psychology is the trend, everyone assumes happiness at work comes from everyone singing kumbaya and holding hands all day long. Okay, that might be slightly exaggerated, perhaps a biased perspective on my end, but you get the point. Work environments are tamed, and the perception that people should always get along has created a delusion that harms more than it helps. In the global payroll environment, where people only reach out to you when something is wrong, living with false expectations leads to constant stress, resentment, and unproductive work relations.

The Painful Truth

The running joke in many households across the world is that no relationship is more challenging for a wife than that with her mother-in-law. There are books written, movies made, and countless stories about the mother-in-law and how miserable she makes her daughter-in-law's life whenever she visits. And yet, on each visit, both women have to make their relationship work somehow because their long-term happiness and the family's longevity depend on these two personalities figuring out a way to hold things together, no matter how they feel about each other's peculiarities. There's a lesson here for us at payroll because our interactions and working relations with the various people needed to run the payroll process, as presented in this book, require plenty of partnership. Reading this book ought to have given you the necessary tools and skills to make developing healthy partnerships a little less straining. And just as the mother-in-law and the wife recognize the importance of getting along despite their differences, you and your partners must find ways to focus on accomplishing the tasks.

A while back, I was brought into a company to assist the CFO and CEO of the organization in fighting an ongoing, heated battle with a vendor company that they felt was an absolute nightmare to work with. The problem escalated to include lawyers, and we all knew it would be a bloody fight if we didn't get to the root issue sooner rather than later. At first, I thought the primary problem was technical, but after some probing and digging, it became evident that this was more of a personal distaste than actual service dissatisfaction. It was the tale of the mother-in-law, except this time, it was in the workplace with two guys sitting across from each other. The vendor's performance was sufficient and met all their contractual obligations. Furthermore, the cost of getting out of said contract was unacceptable to the leadership team because it was running into the millions of euros. So I called a meeting with both parties and had them face each other in a boardroom. We went through the pros and cons of terminating the contract, and I looked the CFO straight in the eye and said, "You either pay the price of terminating this contract early, or you grow up and learn to work with this vendor. Allowing personal feelings and biases to get in the way of doing business is bad for the organization." That was the end of that dispute.

In your function, you don't have the luxury to choose your partners, and you don't have the luxury of discarding them out of personal distaste because you need your partners to get payroll out on time; failure to do so means your customers suffer.

Are you emotionally mature enough to handle the truth? I promise you, it will liberate you. The fact is, you don't need to like someone, and they don't need to like you for something productive to come out of that professional interaction. Friendships and partnerships in the workplace are not mutually exclusive. There are many people I've successfully worked with in the past that I couldn't stand. Their personalities were off-putting, and I would have never invited them to a weekend BBQ at my home, but you couldn't tell because, when it came to getting the job done, I was, first and foremost, a professional. The mission is what I was committed to. I recognized that forging a work partnership had nothing to do with becoming friends. As long as I needed that person to accomplish my job, I would find a way to work well together. This mindset continues to serve me well. I hope you cultivate the same. But let's break down what partnership means and the difference between teamwork and partnerships so you can reframe your approach.

The Difference between Your Team Member and Your Work Partner

A partner is a crucial ally (usually outside the payroll function) with whom you share a vested interest. Regardless of your personal sentiments, biases, and preferences, you are required to wholeheartedly commit to the partnership because there are always high stakes in play, and most of the time (especially in the case of global payroll), you stand to lose the most if you're not committed all the way. However, a team member takes your responsibilities a step further. It's not just about collaborating with them; you also bear the burden of looking out for their well-being. In a sense, you become accountable for their success, and the more you nurture and support them, the greater your overall performance in the function of payroll. Often, emotions can become entangled in this type of relationship. On the other hand, a partner doesn't necessarily entail an emotional connection; it's more about a strategic alliance.

It's imperative to underscore that, in the complex world of global payroll, personal affinities or emotions aren't prerequisites for forging effective partnerships. In fact, the essence of partnership in payroll transcends personal feelings. The global payroll process is a multifaceted orchestration where numerous elements must harmonize to ensure success. It's a tapestry where various threads converge to create the whole. You cannot be a payroll virtuoso in isolation. The intricacies of payroll demand collaboration, teamwork, and partnerships.

The ability to run a successful payroll each time the calendar resets hinges on synchronizing different departments, properly integrating the right software and technology, and complying with ever-evolving regulations. So, while emotions might become entangled in some of your internal relations with team members, it's pivotal to remember that payroll partnerships are fundamentally strategic alliances.

You don't have to like everyone you work with, but you must respect their role in the greater payroll ecosystem. Their success is inherently tied to yours, and your mission is not a one- man/one-woman show. For the payroll function to thrive, partnerships must thrive. The synergy of these partnerships is what sets the stage for seamless payroll processes, accurate calculations, and timely distributions. Ultimately, it's not about whether you like every partner you encounter but whether you can work together effectively to ensure payroll runs like a well-oiled machine. But how do you stay motivated and focused when dealing with less-than-pleasant partners?

Staying Focused on Your Goal

Have you ever thought about what you aim for when you do payroll? Who matters most in this payroll journey? A great payroll manager would quickly tell you it's the employees. And they'd be absolutely right. The key is knowing why you're in the payroll game and what keeps you going, even when things get tough. Think of it this way: Your mission is to ensure your customers—employees—get their hard-earned money on time every month. This money isn't just numbers on a paycheck; it's what puts food on their table, covers their mortgage, pays for tuition, and takes care of bills. It's how they make their lives work. Remember this every time you work with partners from other departments or outside vendors. These partnerships are like your backup squad on the battlefield, helping you win the payroll battle. The end goal is to make sure employees get their money on time so they can keep their lives running smoothly. It's a powerful mission that gives meaning to your everyday payroll tasks. Building strong partnerships is like having a superpower. It's not just about doing your part; it's about ensuring everyone else does their part too. When you work closely with others, it's like having a team of superheroes.

Now, how can you build these powerful partnerships?

It's all about communication. That's why we started with lessons on cultivating qualities that would prime you for this particular role. Be open, clear, and KPI-focused with every interaction. Let your partners know what you need and understand what they need. Respect each other's roles and be mindful of cultural barriers, avoiding biases that would be counterproductive to the task at hand. After all, you're on the same team. And before you end each meeting, always circle back to get feedback and to ensure the person understands your message as you meant it. This collaborative approach will help you achieve your goal of getting employees paid on time.

Problem-Solving in Partnership

You may not have realized this, but the previous chapter was a foundational pillar meant to set you up for success as you forge the various partnerships needed to seamlessly execute the payroll process as presented in this book. Without a highly developed problem-solving skill in your toolbox, you'll keep bumping up against seemingly insurmountable walls. The more proactive you become at problem-solving and taking ownership of customer data, the easier it will be to work with your partners. Consider these two examples and tell me which you'd rather experience.

In the first scenario, you don't take ownership of customer source data, which means you don't control how the data moves. So when HR sends you the data needed to process payroll for the month a little too late, you find yourself in a board room with flaring emotions and frustrated superiors yelling over your incompetence when, in truth, HR sent in the data late and much of it wasn't even accurate. The conversation between you and the HR leader will be more emotional than factual, with plenty of finger-pointing. You'll likely breed more resentment and animosity because they think you're just looking for a scapegoat, and you know their data is corrupted. Now, picture a second scenario with the exact circumstances.

HR still sends in the data a little too late, and despite your best efforts, you miss the deadline. Fortunately, you're indoctrinated into the Payrollmind DNA community, and your process is controlled, tracked, and measured. You've taken ownership of the entire payroll lifecycle following each of the 22 processes disclosed in Chapter 08, so you know how to be accountable for your customer source data and where the chain is broken. You're confident it wasn't your fault, and this time, despite the yelling of the superiors, you have quantifiable data to back up what went wrong. So you calmly turn to HR and thank them for handing in the data, and then you get right into the heart of the problem. The records show that 20% of the data came in too late, 7% was incomplete, and 15% was inaccurate. So despite your best efforts, payroll couldn't be made on time. The best way forward is to understand what can be done from both sides to ensure data is handed in within an agreed-upon timeline and with zero errors. Can you tell the difference between these two examples?

I've been in board rooms on different occasions where both scenarios played out, and let me assure you, when the payroll manager didn't take accountability, no forward movement was possible. In which case, I had to step in and coach them through this way of thinking and problem-solving. Wouldn't it be great if you could no longer live through those scenarios where you feel like you are working with your hands tied behind your back?

Forging Strategic Partnerships

A strong foundation that leads to healthy partnerships comes from cultivating and expressing the qualities that ultimately turn you into an excellent global payroll professional. The more you work on yourself, the better your partnerships become because you approach them from a place of strength and self-awareness. But partnerships don't just happen overnight. And it does require a reality check on your end so that you don't end up being delusional about what it takes to have great partners working with you to accomplish your mission. Your biases and personal preferences about a person (how they look, where they come from, quirks, peculiarities, and more) should never factor into whether or not you can respect them enough to work on the task in front of you. You are always responsible for ensuring people get you what you need to do your best job. What's the right course of action when you recognize someone isn't competent enough to carry their load in the payroll process? My conviction is that in that dire moment when the clock is ticking and you know you're sitting on a time bomb, you must roll up your sleeves and be willing to do whatever it takes to keep things moving so you can meet your 30-day deadline on time. Never stand on the sidelines and watch someone blow up your game because of their incompetence or negligence. If something is jeopardizing your process, jump in, take care of it before things escalate, and after the fact, bring it to the attention of the individual and leadership to determine how to avoid a repeat of the same. That doesn't mean bending over backward month over month to cover up for people who aren't performing. That will only lead to burnout for you and promote unhealthy dependency instead of healthy partnerships. So before we end this chapter, let's cover a simple framework that you can use to build healthy dependency, ensuring you get the support you need and work well with others. A productive partnership has three key elements:

#1: Set the right expectations

Always begin with the assumption that you're working with people who have been placed in their respective positions because they are qualified. They have the right knowledge, skills, and processes necessary to accomplish your aims, address needs, and facilitate successful payroll. With that in mind, your intention must always be to collaborate and work together on a framework of responsibilities and clear expectations. Communicate and align from the start about the objectives, the value you expect, the resources needed, and the timeframes you'll be working with. Your partner is an extension of you within the context of the payroll lifecycle. Whichever of the 22 processes they are assigned to take care of, ensure they are equipped and well-trained on best practices to work adequately on your behalf. What does success look like? What needs should always be prioritized? These are critical to discuss with your partners.

#2: Nurture the partnership

Once there's alignment on objectives, deliverables, and detailed expectations, keep communication easy and open. Go back to the chapter on communication and work on a strategy that will enable you to stay on top of all the various stakeholders with whom you need to maintain open dialogues. Leverage technology where possible so you can be proactive and perhaps even automate things such as reminders and follow-ups where needed. Make it easy for people to access you in case of a delay or emergency. Encourage your partners to keep you in the loop so you get information on arising matters before they escalate. The payroll process can only run smoothly when overlayed with a workflow that facilitates easy communication, so make sure to think ahead and identify any gaps that may get in the way of performance and delivery.

#3: Clarify KPIs and accountability

Internal governance is just as critical to payroll success because, without clarity on the metrics that matter and a sense of accountability, most people just won't deliver what you want when you want it. You must remember that for someone raised and influenced by the German culture, telling them you need a report delivered tomorrow will not be received the same way as for someone raised and influenced by the Spanish culture. To the Germans, today could mean first thing in the morning, whereas the Spanish might assume before the day is done. As such, always be clear and specific about the KPIs that will be monitored, the critical metrics that are being measured against the targets you've set together, and who is accountable for what aspect of the partnership. Of course, there's no point in setting expectations and defining metrics if you and your partner don't review progress and reassess strategy with a regular cadence, so be sure to meet periodically to ensure you're still aligned. In short, transparency, communication, and the courage to call people out when they fall off track are the keys to forging strategic partnerships. You can't afford to be passive or to follow blindly. The initiative is yours to embrace and confidently own because, at the end of the day, the mission is yours. Now, where exactly do these partners come into play in the grander vision of an ideal payroll lifecycle? Let's uncover that next so you can finally start working with the real picture.

Chapter 08:
Global Payroll Lifecycle

The industry standards dictate that payroll is a matter of receiving employee information, processing compensation and benefits, handling exceptions, creating reports, and posting to the general ledger. With but a few exceptions, most would agree that this is what the payroll process is about. I couldn't disagree more. What if I told you that what most consider "running payroll" is actually a third of what the payroll process looks like? And what if the global payroll process, as complex as it typically is, could be more efficiently streamlined, simplified, and sustainably scaled up without breaking the bank? That is what I aim to demonstrate in this chapter. We may get more technical and tactical here, so stick with me because if you fail to grasp the truth about what a strong global payroll process looks like, you'll still run short on performance and execution. Thus far, we have primed your mindset and seeded the right characteristics and qualities necessary to emerge as a powerful global payroll professional. But none of that means much if you can't deliver results. And this is how you deliver.

Perspective Matters

Ever heard that old parable of the blind men and the elephant? It goes something like this. Six blind men meet an elephant for the first time, and each man touches a different part of the elephant and makes predictions about what the elephant is like. Naturally, they all have different perspectives depending on which aspect each man touched. One only touched the side of the animal and declared it smooth and solid like a wall. Another only touched the elephant's limber trunk and declared it to be a giant snake. Another still touched the elephant's pointed tusk and declared it sharp and deadly as a spear. And on and on the story goes. Who was right? Were they all wrong? The truth is, whatever perspective each man had was right, but there was more to it than what they touched. Therefore, they were unable to fully describe what an elephant looked like on their own because they lacked the big picture.

For many years, this problem plagued me because different people described payroll in different ways. I realized this lack of proper perspective helped escalate the complexity and issues of running a smooth payroll. It also weakened accountability, responsibility, and, therefore, the ability to streamline payroll through effective partnerships. After all, if everyone in the room is unclear about where global payroll sits in the larger picture of the organization, it's hard to know when you should step in and take charge, when to share responsibilities, and when to simply mediate. Notice that at no point do I give the option for you as payroll to "step aside" and let others take control because the moment you sit on the sidelines, naively assuming other departments or leaders will prioritize your agenda, is when things tend to go to hell. In the payroll game, we are never passive spectators. We find a way to participate and control what we can because our mission is too critical, and the cost of failure is too high. So, for the past decade, I've been doing everything I can to consolidate all I've learned about payroll since my first day in my teenage years. Connecting the dots helped me recognize that many of us have a tiny understanding of what payroll (especially global payroll) is. We are, in fact, replaying that parable of the six blind men, which causes us to make wrong assumptions. The evolution of our industry demands that we learn to see the big picture, the real picture, the whole picture. And that picture is bigger and more impactful than you thought.

What most still consider payroll is but a third of all that the global payroll process entails. No wonder the solutions break or lack sustainability. If you're not solving issues holistically and addressing the entire ecosystem, then you're not really solving the problem, are you?

My proprietary Payrollmind DNA model educates payroll professionals on their professional growth and introduces the payroll lifecycle clustered into tiers to help our students strategically zoom out and grasp the proper perspective of the entire global payroll process. We begin with the premise that to maximize a tool effectively, one must have sufficient self- awareness and skill to utilize the tool. The payroll lifecycle model is a tool that works best with an executor who has cultivated the Payrollmind DNA for themselves, because only then does one know how to maximize the impact of these tools in achieving one's aim. Makes sense? Fortunately for you, I'm going to walk you through that same model so you can complete this chapter with the right understanding of what it takes to run a global payroll.

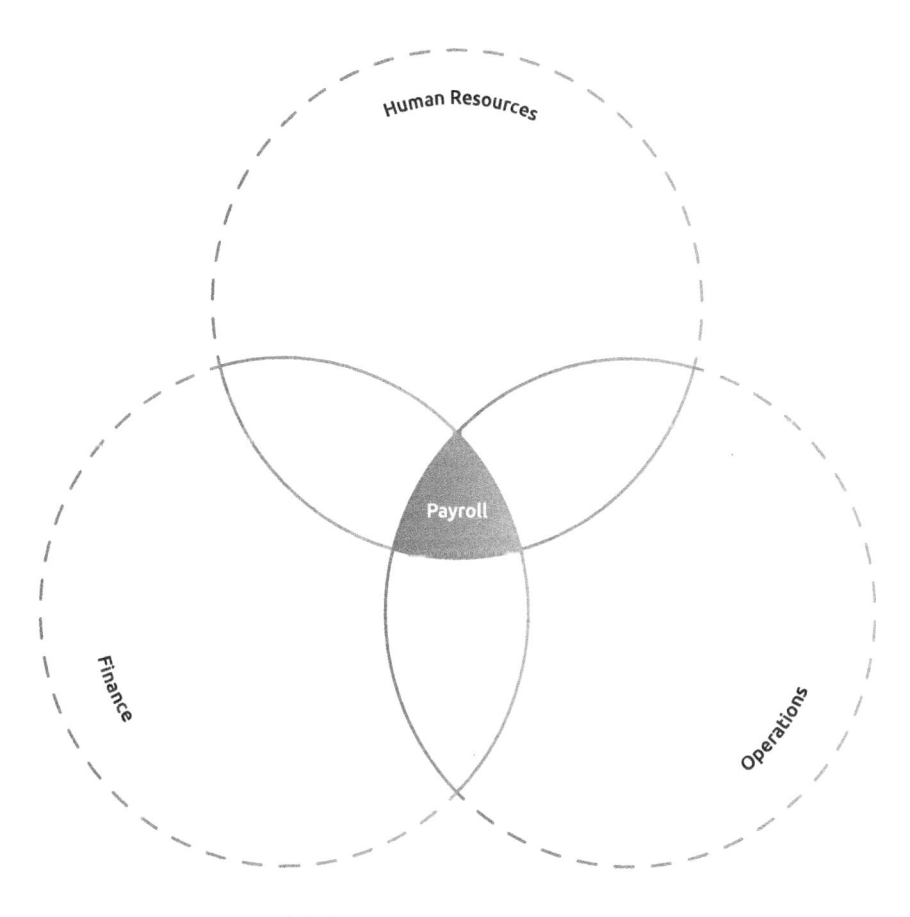

Global payroll: Seeing the bigger picture.

Where global payroll plays best is at the point of intersection between HR (pre-payroll), Finance (post-payroll), and Operations (throughout the entire process from hire to retire). Are you beginning to see just how impactful, influential, and integral your role is to the longevity and success of your organization?

Global Payroll Lifecycle from Start to Finish

The global payroll lifecycle consists of twenty-two essential processes spanning HR, finance, and operations. Our model breaks down and consolidates these processes into four main tiers for optimum transformation and strategic breakthrough. To become a global payroll manager or leader with a bright future, you must recognize the overlap between the three independent functions within your organization and the four strategic tiers that hold the key to improved efficiency, scalability, and compliance. These tiers move from low touch, high volume to high touch, and low volume in all the critical areas of the payroll lifecycle. The real value of our model may be found in this transformative tool that we use to map out and uncover untapped opportunities so we can streamline, simplify, and optimize payroll strategically for the entire organization. This is what global payroll is all about. We must take ownership of the whole payroll lifecycle and simplify the various processes integral to successfully executing payroll.

In the previous chapter, we discussed the importance of recognizing that partnership is integral to your success as a global payroll professional and that you cannot bring your feelings or personal bias into work because your mission is to serve your customers—the employees— with the help of your partners. As it might be evident now, your partners aren't just the vendors and local authorities; they also include the people you need at each touchpoint when going through the twenty-two payroll processes. Without getting into the nitty-gritty of these touchpoints, let's briefly cover what they are, how one hands off to the next, and what you need to start doing to run your payroll more efficiently. At the end of this chapter, you will receive an invitation to join me virtually for a more in-depth discussion should you have questions or if you'd like to dive deeper into the four strategic tiers for transformation within the payroll function.

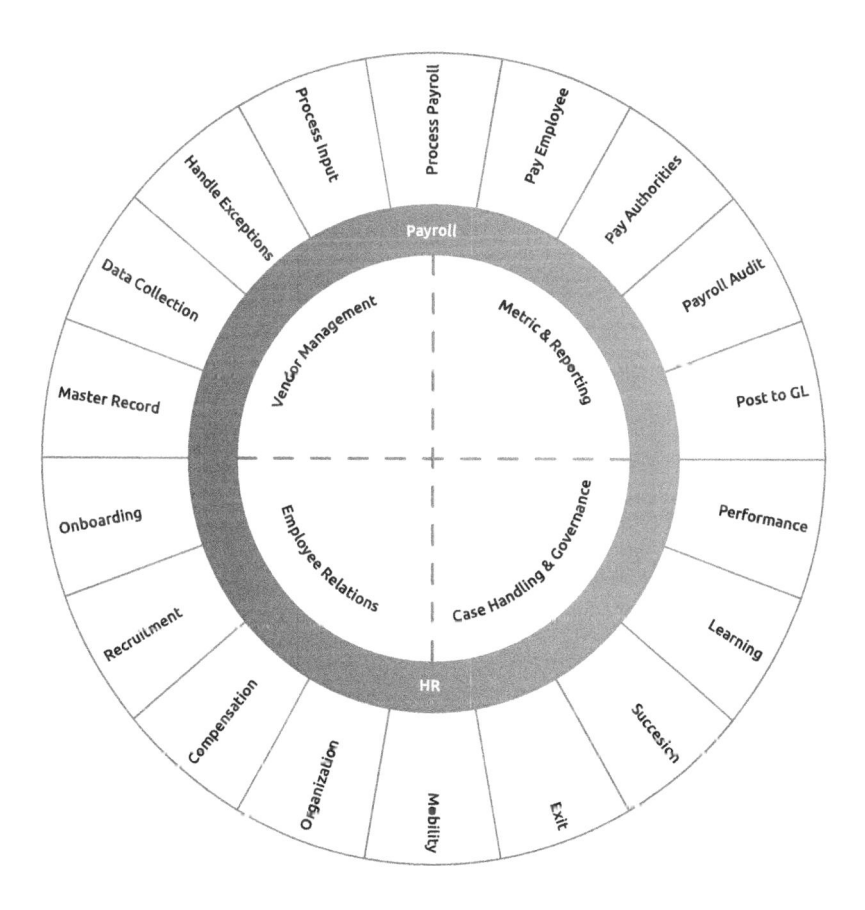

The Global Payroll Lifecycle: 22 Essential HR and Payroll Processes.

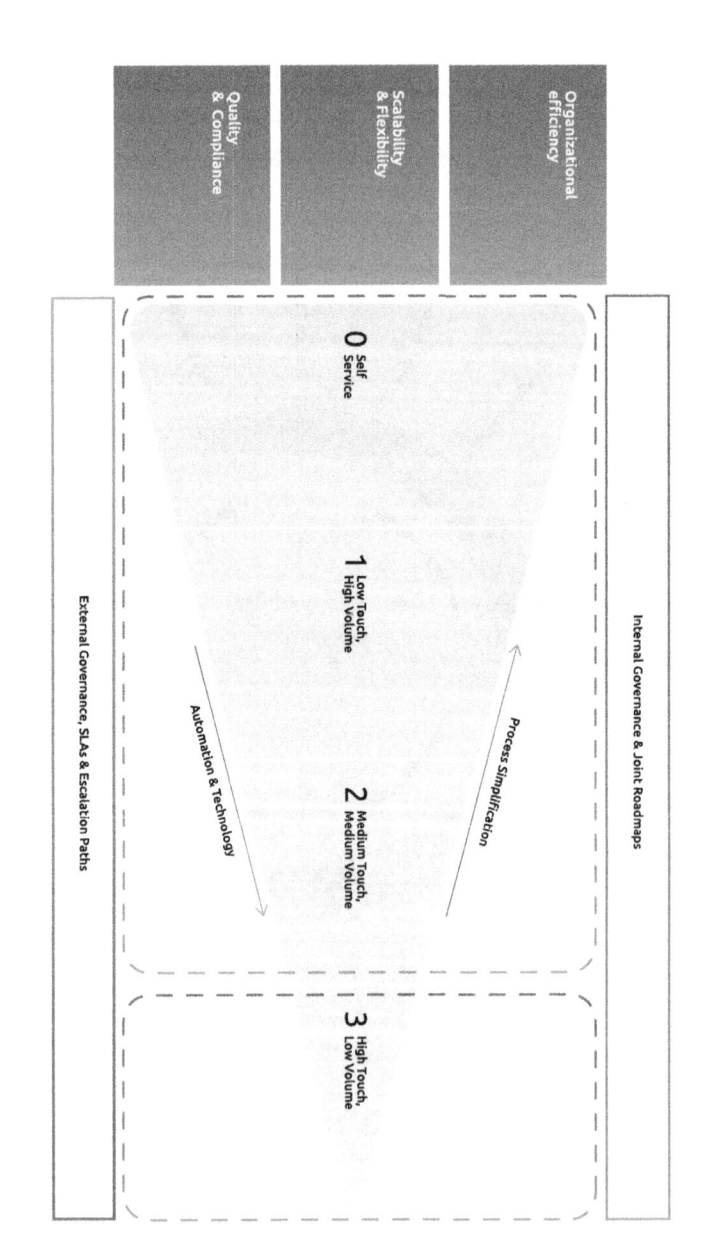

Global Payroll Strategy Framework: Optimize resources, processes, and technology

- **Organizational efficiency**
- **Scalability & Flexibility**
- **Quality & Compliance**

- **0** Self Service
- **1** Low Touch, High Volume
- **2** Medium Touch, Medium Volume
- **3** High Touch, Low Volume

Automation & Technology →
Process Simplification ←

Internal Governance & Joint Roadmaps

External Governance, SLAs & Escalation Paths

The Twenty-Two Processes of the Global Payroll Lifecycle

From compensation, benefits, time, and other HR policies to onboarding, employee record collection, processing payroll, posting on the general ledger, and everything in between, you can already see we're approaching payroll more holistically. We seek to build an ecosystem that puts us in the driver's seat and more in control of the very things that stand to jeopardize our ability to execute the mission. Of the twenty-two processes you've observed in my diagram, I want to emphasize the four that are nonlinear and present at each touchpoint.

These are metrics and reporting, case handling and governance, vendor management, and employee relations. These four tend to be overlooked or mismanaged until it's too late. Yet without perfect alignment and ongoing monitoring, the payroll process will continue to fall apart, regardless of the software and technology your organization invests in. The more proactive you are at ensuring these four processes are under your purview, the easier it becomes to spot red flags and anomalies that could hinder payroll for the month. How does one do this?

It begins with that decision to take ownership of the payroll lifecycle and the recognition that, as a global payroll manager, you must care about policies and procedures just as much as you care about source data. The creation and execution of policies and procedures affect the payroll lifecycle, as does the gathering, recording, and movement of source data. Connecting the dots between policies, procedures, and data creates a robust foundation for your process. Each process in the payroll lifecycle is a piece of the puzzle, and ensuring they fit together seamlessly is part of your job description. The beauty of this approach is that you can tackle each component of your payroll lifecycle puzzle one piece at a time, beginning with any process, simplifying, streamlining, and scaling it to your heart's content (with the help of your strategic partners in those relevant departments), and with each optimization, the positive effects will reflect in other areas of your ecosystem as well. The goal is to operate with precision and foresight, catch issues before they escalate, and ensure your global payroll ecosystem thrives. To achieve this, the four nonlinear processes—metrics and reporting, case handling and governance, vendor management, and employee relations—act as your early warning system, detecting inconsistencies and deviations from the plan. Let's explore each a little further.

#1: Metrics and Reporting

Metrics: Metrics and key performance indicators (KPIs) are the compass of your global payroll journey. They provide invaluable insights into the health of your payroll process. By consistently measuring and monitoring key metrics, you can spot trends, identify issues, and make data-driven decisions. Some essential metrics include:

- **Accuracy Rate:** This metric measures the percentage of error-free payments in your payroll. It's a fundamental gauge of how well your process is performing.
- **Timeliness:** Timeliness metrics assess how quickly payroll is processed. Delays can lead to frustration and compliance issues, making it a crucial metric to watch.
- **Compliance:** Ensure you meet all legal and regulatory requirements in each jurisdiction. Noncompliance can lead to expensive fines and legal issues.

Reporting: Effective reporting is all about turning data into actionable insights. Regular reports allow you to communicate the status of payroll to stakeholders and make informed decisions. Reports should be clear, concise, and tailored to the needs of your audience, which could include senior leaders, finance teams, and local HR.

#2: Case Handling and Governance

Case Handling: Efficient case handling ensures that discrepancies, disputes, and issues are addressed promptly. You need a structured system to receive, track, and resolve cases. This includes everything from employee inquiries about their payslips to addressing payroll errors. Establishing a clear workflow for case handling helps maintain employee satisfaction and mitigate larger problems down the road.

Governance: Governance refers to the rules, processes, and structures that govern the entire payroll process. It's about ensuring that everyone involved follows the agreed-upon policies and procedures. Effective governance reduces risks, enhances compliance, and keeps the process on track. It includes documenting processes, having clear approval hierarchies, and ensuring adherence to policies.

#3: Vendor Management

Vendor Selection: Choosing the right payroll service provider is paramount. Evaluate potential vendors based on their track record, technology, global capabilities, and cost-effectiveness. The wrong vendor can lead to numerous headaches down the line.

Contract Management: Once you've selected a vendor, meticulous contract management is crucial. Your contract should spell out service levels, responsibilities, and penalties for noncompliance. Regularly

review vendor performance to ensure they meet their obligations.
Dispute Resolution: Disputes with vendors can disrupt your payroll process. Having a clear procedure for resolving disputes and discrepancies is essential. This should include a defined escalation path and a mechanism for holding the vendor accountable.

#4: Employee Relations

Grievance Handling: Establish a process for employees to raise concerns and grievances related to their payroll. Make sure this process is transparent, confidential, and responsive. Swiftly addressing employee concerns helps maintain morale and trust.

Open Communication: Effective employee relations involve maintaining open lines of communication. Regularly inform employees about payroll changes, tax updates, and other relevant matters. This can be done through emails, newsletters, or even webinars, depending on the size and structure of your organization.

Feedback Mechanism: Create a feedback mechanism where employees can provide input on the payroll process. Their insights can be invaluable in fine-tuning the process and ensuring it meets their needs.

Incorporating these four critical processes into your global payroll strategy ensures that you have a comprehensive and responsive system in place. They act as the vanguard, preventing issues from spiraling out of control and helping you maintain a well-functioning payroll process.

Claiming Your Seat at the Table

Imagine for a moment that you run payroll for a multinational organization with employees working in fifty different regions of the world. Leadership decides it's a great idea to promote health and wellness by introducing a new wellness scheme that gives each employee a new bicycle. It's a seemingly simple initiative with well-meaning intentions, but just imagine the logistics of executing such a policy. The HR leader in charge of this should recognize that introducing and implementing such a policy has financial, procedural, fiscal, legal, and compliance implications that must be addressed before moving forward. Therefore, it is wise to bring all relevant partners and stakeholders together for a collaborative session to determine the best way to execute such a policy. In the United States, employees may readily welcome this gift and see it as a timely initiative given the cultural trends toward wellness, but in parts of Europe where certain taxes apply, employees might be a little reluctant to accept this policy because no one wants a few hundred euros to come out of their pocket for a gift they never asked for. Your Indian customers might not be interested at all in a 1,000- dollar bicycle and would rather receive different alternatives better suited to their environment. That introduces tension in your role and how you run and implement this for your customers.

Payroll deserves to be part of this conversation and has earned a seat at that boardroom meeting because it is payroll that can determine whether the local authorities in these respective regions have the capacity to handle such a policy and which countries may introduce unfavorable terms that would likely create a financial backlash or low satisfaction score for the employees. And since we're talking about a hefty financial investment to execute the scheme, it's worth addressing these concerns during the conception phase of the policy. The legal team might also have their concerns because, despite the fact that, from a tax perspective, the US employees are covered, it might be a point of vulnerability for the organization to issue bikes to employees in New York, where they are likely to get injured on their commute. So, can the company be liable for this, or to what extent can legal cover the organization should the policy go through? The bottom line is that these departments all need to actively participate but seldom do. Behind closed boardrooms, decisions are made without the big picture or the right leaders in place to add their perspectives to ensure the organization is covered and everyone benefits from policymaking.

As the payroll manager, understanding that you wield the power to inform leadership on what's feasible and risky and what alternatives there are to accomplishing the same objectives should empower you to step up in your role. That means taking ownership of the entire ecosystem and understanding how policies and procedures are established and executed internally and externally. It also requires you to understand the implications of said policies from a data perspective because often, in global payroll, you might be dealing with an employee working in a foreign country as a resident but still registered under their local payroll system. So, for instance, in the example of the company bike, you might have an American employee working in France who would like to receive the 1,000-dollar bike but is required to pay tax benefits out of their pocket. And in the likely event that this American citizen is still filed under the American payroll yet works in France, how would the data move? Where would it be stored? Who is responsible for ensuring accuracy in updating the data to reflect the new policy? Who is responsible for ensuring people don't take advantage of this new policy and that those who don't want additional taxes or the bike can receive an alternative option better suited to their needs? Does HR take all the responsibility? Should you? These are the conversations that must happen before executing any new policy. And what if you realized that in certain countries, it would be best to introduce an alternative solution (instead of a bike) that employees would receive more favorably? Would you have the courage to speak up and call out the need to also involve the marketing department in running internal campaigns that educate the employees first? Or would you passively wait for employee complaints to kick and watch HR throw fits or rage after the fact?

I'm not saying taking a holistic approach to building a payroll ecosystem is easy. It will be painstakingly hard, especially in the beginning when you start breaking down the silos of each of these departments, but the effort is worthwhile in the long run when you finally establish an ecosystem that fosters a healthy payroll lifecycle. It's easy to put band-aids on things and to focus on short-term solutions that help you make payroll in the immediate interim. That's what the average payroll professional does. But sooner rather than later, the leaks, delays, inaccuracies, and blind spots will wear you down, no matter how hardworking you are. Your job is to be a professional problem solver, not a first aid worker. And you will never truly unlock your potential and demonstrate all you are capable of if you're constantly bogged down in daily fires that prevent you from strategic long-term thinking and sustainable growth. Therefore, it is in your best interest (not just the organization's) to start developing a thriving ecosystem where all twenty-two processes work cohesively and in unity. Get a plan in place immediately to begin this project. Make a business case that enables leadership and all major stakeholders to understand the value of supporting your cause to simplify and streamline your organization's payroll process. Reread my introduction and wear that strategic hat so you can zoom out far enough to start with an operating model that factors in all the different tiers that are ideal—from low touch, high volume to high touch, and low volume in all the critical areas of the payroll lifecycle. The strategic overview of how you move from global to local enables you to develop the right tactical moves and build a case around automation, technology, and how each of the twenty-two processes can work together at scale to simplify and streamline how the organization runs payroll.

Now, in case you're hesitant about how to actually get buy-in, rest easy. We have a chapter on building influence that's meant to help you become a positive and powerful force within your organization. Take a deep breath. We've gone deep and technical in this chapter; naturally, you might have questions. Perhaps you want a deep dive into my transformative strategy framework. If so, I invite you to accept an invitation to reach out and discuss a strategy session for you and your team. Here, we will use the framework to uncover opportunities to optimize your global payroll lifecycle. Visit *www.payrollminds.com* to get in touch.

Chapter 09:
Building Influence

Your role as a global payroll manager is pivotal to your organization because you're managing the lifeblood of any business—the payroll. The mission you've chosen to accept is to ensure that every employee is compensated accurately and on time—an essential task that often goes unnoticed until something goes wrong. But behind the scenes, you wield immense power that you can harness for the greater good. Influence is not about seeking the spotlight, collecting popularity points, or bending every decision to your will. Instead, it's about leveraging your expertise, voice, and actions to make your department and your role more widely recognized, appreciated, and respected. It's about ensuring that the significance of payroll in the grand scheme of things is acknowledged and valued.

The skills we covered, from communication to problem-solving to learning how to work with and win over partnerships so your mission continues strong, are all part of building and demonstrating your influence. We began this journey by spotlighting the importance of knowing who you are and working to cultivate your highest and best version of yourself. If you ask me, that's the prerequisite to building influence because unless you know and act from your true self, you can't really have influence in any room. Imposter syndrome and many of the issues that people report, like burnout or "feeling like a fraud," stem from a poor foundation of building influence. One can never positively influence another if they lack a fundamental understanding of who they are, what makes them tick, and what they value. As counterintuitive as it may seem, the more time you spend cultivating your Payrollmind DNA through the lens of knowing yourself, the easier it will be to understand and influence others.

The Paradox of Influence

There's a common misconception I must debunk before going further: influence does not equate to having every idea or agenda you propose adopted without question. In reality, your path to becoming an influential figure within your organization will be riddled with instances where senior leadership may not embrace your suggestions. And that's okay. It's essential to understand that this does not reflect your worth or the quality of your ideas. Instead, it's a testament to the complexities of decision-making, differing viewpoints, and organizational dynamics. I can share a commonly recurring personal experience within my consulting firm where a team leader presents a proposal to the leadership that some of us disagree with. After I listen to different views, I may choose not to move forward with the team leader's suggestion. That doesn't make her bad at her job. While she might be slightly disappointed, I expect she realizes that her opinion matters to me as the company's CEO. Still, there's a lot more I need to think about before jumping into new initiatives. My people are comfortable voicing their suggestions, expressing their concerns, and disagreeing with me when needed. So, even if ideas aren't immediately embraced or implemented, the ability to seed new concepts that could be addressed in the future is something I encourage and value at my firm.

Speak Up and Make Your Case

Building influence involves being willing to voice your opinions and advocate for your ideas, even in the face of possible resistance. It's about being a confident and thoughtful contributor to your organization's decision-making process. Be bold in expressing your viewpoints, as long as you do so respectfully and constructively. Your ability to speak up, share your expertise, and make a compelling case, regardless of the outcome, is a testament to your commitment to the organization's success. If you're introverted and uncomfortable using your voice, let the data you've gathered through your newly streamlined payroll process do the talking for you. In the previous chapter, I revealed the same payroll lifecycle framework that we deploy to Fortune 500 companies because I'd like you to be fully equipped to make your case backed by real data. If you find yourself at odds with the CEO regarding changes in payroll policies, disagreeing with the proposed approach that you feel would lead to inefficiencies is best voiced with a data-driven argument. Only then will you keep emotions at bay and avoid creating resentment because people cannot argue with data-backed concerns. It also makes it easier to offer suggestions and alternatives that could help derive the same objective that senior leadership desires. Will it happen that sometimes the CEO will still proceed with the original plan despite you speaking up? Of course. But the difference is that your efforts will not be in vain. CEOs always notice, remember, and appreciate anyone who is a proactive participant and problem solver. You'll notice over time that you get more invitations to be involved in strategic conversations regarding the growth of the company.

Authentically Vulnerable and Yet Impenetrable

Authentic influence is a delicate balance of paradoxes, one of which lies in the need to be both vulnerable and impenetrable. On the surface, this may seem contradictory, but it's an essential aspect of building influence with integrity. To influence authentically, you must first connect with others on a human level. Vulnerability is the bridge that allows you to relate to your colleagues, gain their trust, and establish a genuine connection. When you're open about your experiences, struggles, and even your failures, you become relatable. People find it easier to trust and connect with someone who is real, someone who has faced challenges and has been shaped by their experiences. Your willingness to be vulnerable shows that you're not an infallible authority figure but a fellow human who understands work and life's complexities. By sharing your vulnerabilities, you create an environment where others feel safe doing the same, fostering deeper and more meaningful connections.

While vulnerability is vital, protecting your integrity and maintaining boundaries are equally important. In this context, being impenetrable means guarding against actions or situations that could compromise your principles or the mission you're dedicated to. This paradox of influence implies that while you open up about your experiences and challenges, you remain steadfast in your commitment to the mission. It's crucial to be transparent without divulging confidential information or engaging in behaviors that could tarnish your reputation. When you strike this balance, you become a trustworthy source of guidance and support.

It may seem challenging, but knowing when to be vulnerable and when to be impenetrable is a skill you'll need to learn, and you can only get better with practice. Share personal and professional experiences that others can relate to, but avoid divulging sensitive or confidential information. Your goal is to connect on a human level, not to compromise your integrity. The more clarity you have on boundaries, expectations, and responsibilities, the easier it will be to maintain this delicate balance that helps you build influence. You must know when to say no and when to mediate relationships across departments or with team members who aren't seeing eye to eye. You need to diffuse heated conversations and redirect conversations toward the mission and your goals from a place of compassion and empathy. And you must work on demonstrating consistency in your actions and words. The more reliable and trustworthy you are, the easier it will be for people to trust you. Being a confident, assertive payroll professional is possible even if you don't consider yourself naturally charismatic or extroverted. The vulnerable, compassionate side that causes you to share a few anecdotes here, when diffusing a situation while still ensuring your agenda moves forward, can be a great way to continuously build upon your influence without elbowing others as you climb higher. And since you're working hard to gain more control over the entire payroll lifecycle, which involves various departments, this is a skill you'll find most valuable throughout your career.

Breaking Down Cross-Departmental Silos

Winning the respect of others and thereby establishing influence in their hearts and minds comes down to a few simple qualities. It's about demonstrating that you are honest, competent, trustworthy, reliable, and more committed to your mission than playing office politics. The people you work with must perceive you as the kind of professional who gives no attention to petty emotional issues that often entangle office relationships. They need to feel that you hold everyone accountable for doing their best job because you're also accountable for doing your best job and completing the mission each month. If you've watched any of the *Mission Impossible* films, one of the striking aspects of Ethan Hunt is the fact that everyone around him knows that he will get the mission done. They never doubt him for a moment. And so, despite all the many setbacks the team faces or the dangers and the impossible feats and personal struggles they may encounter along the way, one thing remains the same. Each member comes through for Ethan Hunt because they believe in his commitment to the mission. That's where his influence comes from. In a sense, you want to draw inspiration from Ethan's character and figure out a way of demonstrating to the people in your world that your mission is what matters and that you do everything you can to work with everyone necessary to get the job done.

If you recall, Chapter 08 covered the twenty-two processes of the payroll lifecycle, all of which span across three different departments: finance, HR, and operations. We shared the secret sauce that would make you a positive force for good as the last blocks that few ever think about, which ultimately meant that you'd need to forge your payroll sword at the point of intersection between the three departments so you can break down the silos that often inhibit your ability to run payroll. Building influence across finance, HR, and operations is the big challenge for this chapter. The ability to understand what each of these departments needs and the willingness to align those needs with your agenda is one of the best ways to start building the right kind of influence. You're not required to use tricks and manipulation or change your behavior, as that would be a betrayal to your own self. It's also not about becoming a people pleaser, always bending over backward and letting people walk all over you just so they can deliver what you need. Instead, it's about having the courage to apply the qualities learned in this book and becoming more of who you really are. Your agenda never changes, but how you present it to each department, keeping in mind their needs, matters because it helps them see why working together is a win-win.

Navigating Office Politics while Building Influence

Office politics typically involve activities such as backstabbing, scheming, and maneuvering to gain power for personal benefit. These actions often undermine trust and can be detrimental to both individuals and the organization as a whole. On the other hand, building influence centers around authenticity, honesty, and a commitment to the organization's success. It's about earning respect through your actions and creating a network of trust built on the merits of your expertise and dedication to the mission.

I have always approached the workplace with the belief that one can navigate office politics without actively participating in them. My personal philosophy is to lead by example, focusing on open and honest communication and always prioritizing the mission over personal gain. This approach has, at times, cost me opportunities. I recall years ago, while working at a multinational organization, where my inability and unwillingness to play office politics with the CFO at that time caused me to hand in my resignation. We just knew the situation was irreparable, and when it came down to it, the organization was always going to choose him over me, so I bowed and graciously made my exit. Despite some of these unpleasant moments, for the most part, my approach has allowed me to build lasting influence within the many organizations I've worked in since, because I built my influence based on trust and respect. And here is where I must reiterate the importance of genuinely establishing effective communication and working on trust internally with your team and across all departments. Teams that report low trust tend to have plenty of office politics.

Consider the Navy Seal and how much their teams have to trust each other in every mission. They work as a single unit to get impossible missions accomplished. Each assignment is usually a life-and-death situation, and if they didn't trust each other 100%, their chances of survival greatly diminished. How much "office politics" do you support a Navy Seal team indulging in?

I would guess little to none. Trust and influence, therefore, go hand in hand, even for us in global payroll. You may not realize it, but the work we put into running a global payroll is unlike that of any other department. We are the only business function where the consequences of our actions or inactions carry the greatest weight and could bring about the greatest catastrophe. Think about it. Suppose the marketing department botches a campaign, and the company fails to meet its target for that quarter. In that case, there would be plenty of frustrated leaders and a very unhappy CEO. Still, it's unlikely to wreak as much havoc as employees not getting paid for a month, as that would literally bring the organization to a standstill. For many reading this book, the struggles in the payroll department and the lack of influence are not primarily due to office politics. Lack of influence where it matters is often a symptom of a more profound issue: the inability to communicate effectively and gain buy-in for your vision. The truth is that office politics often thrives when people choose their words and actions based on what they think others want to hear rather than focusing on what is necessary to accomplish their mission. Instead of engaging in negative office politics, focus on your work and your goals. Rise above pettiness, and let your actions speak louder than any rumor or gossip. Even when faced with pressure to conform, stay true to your principles. Compromising your integrity for short-term gains can erode trust in the long run. Keep your mission and goals front and center in your decision-making. When your colleagues see your unwavering dedication to the organization's success, they are more likely to align with your vision.

Strategies for Building Influence

Building influence is an ongoing process that requires a strategic approach. Here are some practical suggestions based on our Payrollmind DNA framework to help you become a more influential global payroll manager:

Leverage Your Expertise: Your deep knowledge of global payroll and related processes is a valuable asset. Use it to your advantage. Share your expertise with others, and be the go-to person for information and guidance in your area. When you consistently demonstrate your expertise, others naturally turn to you for advice and support.

Build Relationships: Cultivating strong relationships is at the heart of influence. Take the time to get to know your colleagues and superiors. Understand their goals, motivations, and challenges. Building rapport can create a sense of trust and mutual respect, which are fundamental to influence.

Effective Communication: Communication is a cornerstone of influence. Practice active listening and articulate your ideas clearly and confidently. Tailor your communication style to your audience, and be open to feedback. Remember that effective communication is a two- way street, and the ability to understand others is just as important as being understood. Go back and reread the chapter on effective communication once more.

Lead by Example: Lead through your actions and behaviors. Demonstrate your commitment to the organization's values and mission. Your efforts should align with your words, reinforcing your credibility and integrity. When your team sees you embody the values you promote, it sets a powerful example.

Adapt and Be Flexible: Influence often involves compromise and adaptability. Be open to different viewpoints and willing to adjust your strategies when necessary. Flexibility is a sign of maturity and can help you navigate organizational challenges and changes more effectively.

Patience and Persistence: Building influence takes time. Be patient and persistent, and don't be discouraged by setbacks. In the long run, your consistent efforts will be a positive force for good that will pay off.

Remember, as a global payroll manager, your role is not to become entangled in the web of office politics. Your primary objective is to ensure that the payroll department is recognized as an integral component of your organization's success. Office politics can be a distraction, but it doesn't have to define your journey. Stay true to who you are and live by your principles and values. Be open, honest, and as transparent as you can be while focusing on the mission. The trust you earn, the respect you command, and the influence you wield will all be based on your unwavering commitment to your principles, goals, and the organization's mission. Authentic influence transcends fleeting alliances and manipulative tactics. It is a force for good that leaves a lasting imprint on your colleagues and the entire organization.

You can be the guide, the inspiration, and the catalyst for the change your organization needs.

Part 3

Chapter 10:
Overcoming Challenges

In and out of the office, life is a journey filled with obstacles, setbacks, and unforeseen twists. Challenges are like the sand traps on a golf course; they may seem daunting, but you can navigate them successfully with the right approach. In fact, overcoming challenges is not only a testament to our resilience but an essential factor in building influence within our organizations and enhancing our problem-solving skills. I've often said that global payroll is about solving one problem after another. In other words, we are professional problem solvers. This means challenges are the norm, not the exception, in our work experience. Whether it's a demanding project that keeps stalling because HR and finance can't find a middle ground, a tough decision to make with a vendor, a new policy that jeopardizes employee compensation, or an unexpected crisis that brings the entire organization to a standstill, these circumstances are opportunities to demonstrate what we're made of. They're the proving grounds where leaders and team players are forged. When you consistently rise to the occasion, navigate hurdles, and emerge stronger on the other side, you build your reputation as a reliable, resilient, and influential individual. Others begin to look to you for guidance and inspiration because they know you can weather the storm. This is where the connection between problem-solving, building influence, and the ability to overcome challenges becomes clear.

You're not just a talker but a doer; others cannot help but recognize the value you bring to the organization.

The Resilience Factor

Resilience is the cornerstone of overcoming challenges. It's the ability to bounce back when faced with adversity, the capacity to adapt to change, and the determination to keep moving forward despite setbacks. Building resilience is not a one-time event but an ongoing journey. Most people assume my success, influence, and confidence come from always winning and getting my way. Having high levels of mental, emotional, and spiritual resilience is perhaps the great secret that fuels what others perceive as success and stamina. I have failed more times than I dare count and experienced tremendous pain in various seasons of my life, personally and professionally. The loss, disappointments, and failures of my life are just as essential to my success as my wins. So, I don't want you to end this book with a false perception of what it takes to win in your career. The more problems you solve, the more you will encounter moments that bring you to your knees. It's not a question of avoiding those moments or attempting to attain perfectionism. Instead, it's about learning to own the mistakes, failures, and disappointments and picking yourself up as quickly as possible. Think like an athlete. Don't worry about how many misses it takes to play like a champion because, at the end of the day, people just want to know that you will ultimately get the final win.

Developing High Levels of Mental Endurance

Unfortunately, even though this life skill serves everyone, we're never taught mental endurance in school. And while I don't claim to be an expert on the topic, I have some insights from personal experience and from studying the athletes that inspire me. So consider applying the following mindset:

1. **Embrace Failure:** Failure is not a dead end but a stepping stone. Embrace your mistakes, learn from them, own them, and use them as a foundation to build future success.
2. **Stay Positive:** Cultivate a positive mindset. Maintain a can-do attitude and focus on solutions rather than dwelling on past problems.
3. **Set Small Goals:** Break down larger challenges into smaller, manageable goals. Achieving these mini-goals boosts your confidence and builds forward momentum.
4. **Positive Self-Talk:** Your internal dialogue can significantly impact your mental state. Pay attention to the way you speak to yourself during challenging times. Replace negative or self-critical thoughts with positive

and affirming messages. Remind yourself of your strengths and previous successes.
5. **Seek Support:** Don't be afraid to seek help or guidance when necessary. A support system can provide valuable insights and encouragement. Consider joining a community of like-minded individuals who can help keep you accountable and share your journey.

Obstacles Are Stepping Stones

Overcoming challenges isn't just about pushing through adversity. It's about changing your perspective. Instead of viewing obstacles as stumbling blocks, see them as stepping stones on your path to success.

When you encounter a challenge, ask yourself, "What can I learn from this?" This simple shift in mindset can turn a seemingly insurmountable obstacle into an opportunity for growth and development. For example, if the head of HR disagrees with the finance department and that's causing a recurring delay, that could cost you greatly. You could passively wait for them to work things out, which may or may not happen in time. Or you could step up, take ownership of the payroll lifecycle, and become a mediator to clear the issue between them.

That would open up the conversation of finding alternatives to the problem that could enable you to leverage technology and streamline the process so both departments no longer need to manually hand over the information you need to do your job. Not only do you help resolve and dissolve a conflict across the departments, but you also push your agenda of streamlining and simplifying payroll for the organization—and all because you decided to face the problem and take ownership, seeing it as an opportunity rather than an obstacle. Each challenge becomes a chance to prove your resilience and problem-solving skills, enhancing your influence within your organization.

When faced with a challenge, don't shy away from it. Embrace it as an opportunity to demonstrate your problem-solving skills. Your ability to analyze issues, develop solutions, and take action is a fundamental component of influence. Colleagues and superiors naturally gravitate toward individuals who provide solutions and drive results. And this doesn't just positively impact your personal growth. It also inspires trust and confidence in those around you. When others see you tackling difficulties with determination and resilience, they're more likely to trust your judgment and follow your lead. Your actions speak volumes about your character and commitment to the organization's success. It also demonstrates your adaptability. Being adaptable is essential for maintaining a competitive edge, and colleagues and superiors are more likely to respect and seek your insights when they perceive you as someone who can navigate change gracefully.

A Learner's Mind

When I first started playing golf, I faced numerous challenges—inconsistent swings, missed putts, and wayward shots into the rough.

But with every round, I viewed these challenges as opportunities to improve. I analyzed my swings, took lessons, and practiced relentlessly. I didn't see the missed putts as failures but as feedback for enhancing my game. Over time, and with a lot of help, I became a more skilled amateur golfer, confident in my abilities to overcome challenges on the course. I applied the same dedication and learner mindset I've used to navigate every big obstacle. As a result, my game improved on the golf course and in other areas, too.

In the business world, just as in golf, challenges are inevitable. How you approach and conquer them defines your character and influence. Your ability to overcome obstacles showcases your resilience, problem-solving skills, and unwavering commitment to the mission.

Building influence is not solely about being the most talented or charismatic person in the room. It's about being the individual people can count on when it matters, who leads with resilience, and who inspires others to stay on track until the mission is complete.

So, as you face the sand traps, water hazards, and bunkers in your professional journey, remember what every golfer knows. Every obstacle is a stepping stone that you can use to step up your game. It's an opportunity to grow, learn, and become a better professional who can not only navigate the course but also lead by example. Your authentic influence, built on a foundation of resilience and problem-solving, will leave a lasting legacy in your organization, shaping its future and contributing to its long-term success.

Chapter 11: Leadership as a Force for Good

A book on global payroll that doesn't lend itself to the topic of good leadership would feel incomplete, in my humble opinion. As I have said in almost every workshop and training I've spoken at, there is no substitute for poor leadership. Our processes can be great, and our technology can be top-notch. We can hire the cream of the crop from the talent pool, but if our internal compass on what it means to lead global payroll fails, it will all be in vain.

Leadership at each level of the organization matters. Since our focus is global payroll, we won't dive into C-suite leadership challenges (and there are many). Instead, we'll focus on empowering you to think and act as a leader, regardless of your title. A problem solver is, by default, a leader because they already possess the qualities of self-sufficiency, independent thinking, courage, commitment, curiosity, and empathy that make a great leader. Leadership isn't optional for a payroll professional. It's a necessity. Therefore, whether you plan to rise to a formally recognized leadership role or not, I encourage you to permit yourself to be a leader in your own right. Your role in managing payroll transcends the tactical aspects of processing paychecks; it's about shaping the success and longevity of your department and the organization. And that will regularly include knowing when to motivate others, resolve conflicts, and keep people accountable so you can move toward mission success.

Team Motivation: The Heart of Leadership

One of the core responsibilities of leadership is motivating your team. Motivation is the engine that drives your department forward, helping it overcome challenges, meet deadlines, and exceed expectations. But it's tough to motivate others in any environment, let alone a fast-paced, pressured environment like a global payroll, where things always go wrong. My insights on team motivation and performance come down to nailing a few fundamental principles that begin with your personal growth. The more work you've done getting clarity on who you are and showing up authentically as that best version of yourself, the easier it will be to support others to perform better. Your clear vision of what the mission is and the role everyone plays in meeting agreed-upon targets is essential. What are your department's goals and objectives? How does each member contribute to the organization's success? Does everyone know the big picture, and are they clear on what they each need to do, plus how their progress will be measured?

When your team understands the vision, their place in it, and the deliverables exactly as you expect, they become more engaged and motivated. Second, this level of clarity is the ability to appreciate, acknowledge, and possibly reward your team for their performance. Get into the habit of offering encouraging words to reinforce the value of hard work around you. After all, everyone likes to know they are valued for their contribution. If your organization isn't keen on employee rewards, consider starting something simple within your department. Even passing on handwritten notes each month can help offer praise to the people who need to know their effort doesn't go unnoticed. That naturally leads to the topic of accountability.

Most people assume that being empowered is only about offering encouragement and praise, but that's only half of the equation. The other side of it comes down to keeping your team accountable. Identifying specific metrics and mapping them to deliverables that each member can live up to, then helping them take ownership of their work, is actually very empowering. It gives one a sense of responsibility and pride because it's easy to track and report on what one contributes to the success of the department and the organization at large. That is what fosters true motivation and a commitment to excellence.

Conflict Resolution

Conflict is an inevitable part of running a global payroll. After all, when dealing with multiple time zones and various cultures across several departments, there's bound to be miscommunication, differing opinions, and misunderstandings. It's not uncommon to find yourself at odds with the HR leader over critical payroll processing decisions. Perhaps there was a recent change in employment law for one of the regions with the highest number of employees. HR might have a different view on how you should address these changes, but you already know much of the leader's concerns are merely that and nothing that should require a drastic change in the current process. This is a common occurrence in many organizations. The problem is that if allowed to escalate, it could lead to a stalemate that affects morale and productivity for the rest of the team members. All of that can be avoided if you immediately confront the issue by candidly discussing and articulating the facts to help the HR leader understand your point of view.

Equally important is allowing the leader to share her anxiety about potential legal ramifications and why she feels she must push for these changes. If you've been implementing the ideas suggested in this book, you'd know having this sit-down is part of effective communication and problem-solving. You don't just want to assure her that your process is sound. You want to back it up with facts and legal proof, if necessary. You may have gone a step further and called in legal to clarify that you're currently compliant. The impact of such an approach is that you'd reach an agreement sooner rather than later. The HR team witnesses your willingness to take ownership of the situation and your ability to collaborate to achieve a shared goal. This conflict, which could have eroded trust, now serves as a catalyst for stronger cooperation and authentic influence.

The bottom line is this: How you handle conflicts as a leader can have a profound impact on your team's morale and cohesion. Here's my recommendation on how to approach it:

1. **Active Listening:** When conflicts arise, take the time to actively listen to all parties involved. Understand their perspectives and concerns. That demonstrates your commitment to resolving the issue fairly.
2. **Objective Analysis:** Your role is to remain impartial, unemotional, and objective. Examine the facts and the impact of the conflict on the team and the organization. Practice what you learned in this book, and be mindful of your biases and preferences so they don't get in the way of you making the proper analysis. What matters is that you can identify the problem and figure out what's not working and what must happen in order for things to move forward.
3. **Facilitate Discussion:** Encourage open and constructive dialogue among the parties in conflict. That provides an opportunity for individuals to express their viewpoints and work toward a resolution. Be open to disagreements and honor everyone's truth, especially when it doesn't match your perspective.
4. **Problem-Solving Approach:** Approach conflicts as problems to be solved, not battles to be won. Seek solutions that are in the best interest of the team and the organization, even if it means compromising.

Cultivating Leadership Qualities

Courage, commitment, and accountability are essential qualities for every global payroll professional looking to become a leader. These are the qualities that form the backbone of effective leadership. Leadership often requires making difficult decisions, confronting challenges, and standing up for what you know is right, even if no one else wants to hear it. In my consulting firm, we refer to it as brutal honesty. It's one of the values we strive to live up to when dealing with clients, talent, and each other. It's always easy to speak your truth and call out what others might try to avoid. Sometimes, the person you will have to disagree with is your boss. And still, I encourage you to practice candor in all your relationships and partnerships. Demonstrating this form of courage is the foundation upon which you can build trust and respect from your team and superiors.

Commitment to living and working in integrity becomes plausible with courage and candor. You turn into a committed leader who is dedicated to the success of the team and the organization. Your unwavering commitment to your role and the mission can and will inspire your team to go the extra mile. Think about what I'm suggesting here. It's not about trying to get a new title added to your current role or asking anyone to make you a leader. This is about leadership by example—the best kind there. And the more you can show up as who you really are, the likelier you are to get your team, partners, and executive leadership to match you in their respective duties.

The Pursuit of Continuous Education

Continuous education, both personally and professionally, is essential to becoming a true force for good within your organization. None of us know it all, and there is no end to the information and knowledge we can acquire. Education is a powerful tool we must continue to use as leverage to enhance our capabilities as payroll professionals. When you commit to learning and development, you send a message to everyone in your world that growth and improvement are ongoing processes. You become a role model, showing that leadership is about evolving, adapting, and striving for excellence.

Leadership as a Force for Good

Leadership is not just about guiding your team; it's about developing and using your influence for the greater good and playing the long game. Decades ago, when I entered payroll, work was very different, and the payroll process was archaic. Evolution in how we work, where we work (whether in the office or remotely), and how many different locations and cultures we work with all add to a very complex payroll process. Five years ago, hybrid environments with a team dispersed all over the world running virtual meetings were almost nonexistent. Today, it has become the new norm. Global payroll must keep up with this evolution. We must keep up with this evolution and strive to shift from a mere business function to a strategic department. With strategy comes the call to facilitate more collaborations and cross-departmental processes. These complex setups that will increasingly become the norm can only work if more payroll professionals take on a more leadership role. The systems and technologies we deploy into our organizations only work if we work them. And we must work with them at a higher level under good communication and leadership conditions.

Whether you're in face-to-face interactions with payroll team members, exchanging emails with a colleague from another department, or assisting a remote worker serving the organization in a different location, you have a chance to demonstrate leadership, regardless of your title. Failure to do so can only perpetuate the internal frustrations plaguing your department. As a global payroll professional, you have the unique opportunity to impact the lives of employees and the entire organization. And since leadership is most effective when driven by a sense of purpose, you must determine for yourself what your purpose will be.

Your contribution as a global payroll leader isn't just processing payrolls; it's about ensuring the financial well-being of your organization's employees. Let your purpose become a powerful motivator and source of direction. When you lead with purpose, you not only inspire your team but also contribute to a meaningful and fulfilling workplace. Isn't that worth putting in the effort to grow?

Conclusion

My first taste of payroll was at the age of fourteen when my dad introduced me to finance. Though not a trained professional, my dad saw a problem that needed solving and challenged me to learn the ropes to build something meaningful for myself. Being the confident go-getter, there wasn't any hesitation that I would make it work. Years later, my journey took me to an incredible company, where I found myself jet-setting around the world, putting in countless hours, and making significant strides in my career. My primary goal back then was to climb the corporate ladder, aiming for the VP position and a seven-figure income in the United States. After all, running a team of over one hundred people from all over the world dealing with cultures vastly diverse from mine had equipped me with everything I needed to step into a big title with a corner office and a view to envy, right?

While my ambitions and actions continued to trailblaze my path of success, life had other plans for me. I still recall the day and the hour my wife and I received the fateful news from the doctors that our infant son wasn't going to make it, and there was nothing the medical field could do to prevent the inevitable. After running around like mad parents for weeks trying to save our son, we finally resolved that it was best to take him home and spend whatever time we had left with our newborn. Although we only had him for four months, that experience changed everything.

A tragic moment—the loss of our son—plunged me into a deep, heart-wrenching darkness. The death of a child is beyond painful. It brings about a kind of suffering that I wouldn't wish on my worst enemy. My family went through a tumultuous season that took a while to reset from, and we all dealt with it in different ways. Some of us (me) opted to pretend that everything was okay enough to jump back into the maniac work life that had become my norm a few weeks after his passing. Part of me assumed I could manage. In fact, I fooled myself into thinking distracting myself with work would be the answer to healing. After all, I was a machine programmed to win.

For years, my modus operandi was getting results and putting in the work, no matter what. So why should this misfortune change anything? Except it did. It changed everything. The loss of my son threw me into a free fall, and as everything went up in the air, a deep void created within forced me to reflect upon my life choices. Who was I? What matters to me in life?

Was I really on the right path? Was I in the right company, and was this company genuinely treating its employees well? Does my work even matter? What do I truly want? Is it the goal of moving to the US and earning seven figures or something else? Why were people at work so depressed? Why did some choose suicide, and how could I not have seen their unhappiness before? What made them so unhappy and powerless? These questions needed answers, and I was no longer satisfied with just getting results and grinding it out.

I fell into a deep depression for a while, and although my organization supported me and my family tremendously, it soon became apparent that change was imminent. The death of my son took something irreplaceable, but it also gave me something. It forced me to reconnect more with my human side.

From Taker to Giver

A part of me that I had long neglected and muted out had a rebirth—thanks to my son. I could no longer play the same role or be that mean machine that everyone knew. I looked at success, winning, and people in a new light and questioned everything I thought was right about running a global payroll. My former interpretation of the company values that I was working to uphold no longer made sense. While enduring this massive change in my life, I suddenly realized that what I loved most about payroll, what got me into payroll as a teenager, was my love for developing people, nurturing and being part of great teams, and making the impossible happen in a way that elevated everyone involved. I had gone into payroll for the people, not the mechanics and spreadsheets, and I needed to find my way back to being who I really am. I'd spent most of my career life internally focused and using my best qualities for success only to advance myself. It was time to stop being a taker and start being a giver.

I came to recognize that developing people and guiding people through the constant changes of payroll, ensuring that they succeed and enjoy themselves through that process, was more important to me than status. So, I decided to forge a new path and begin a new chapter of healing and reinvention, both personally and professionally. It took a while for my family to find that ray of light after that dark season, but we stuck together, and I am deeply grateful to have such an amazing, loving, and strong partner for a wife who handled that entire transition far better than I. I often relied on her strength to get me through the metamorphosis we had to endure. And as I said at the beginning, sometimes things must get really ugly before becoming beautiful. The transformation that enabled me to become the leader, husband, father, and business owner I am today can be directly attributed to the dark twist in my life— a season of utter devastation and crippling pain. While payroll and my company had nothing to do with it, the consequences of the experience altered my approach to payroll for the better.

It was in that season that I realized I wasn't living up to my full potential, and I was missing the key ingredient that makes success worthwhile—the people. My equation was out of order because, for years, I had placed results above my people. Now, I wanted to find a way to place people above results and to make it possible to end up with a success equation that included happy, productive people and desired results. In other words, could I achieve my mission without collateral damage? That set me off on a new adventure—one that is proving to be the most satisfying and rewarding experience yet.

I share this dark and vulnerable side of my journey because I want you to realize that regardless of where you stand now, the only way to have what you truly want in life is for you to work on becoming more of who you really are. Life and business are interconnected, so a shift in your mindset, personal habits, and a commitment to grow as a person directly impacts your performance and opportunities at work. The principles and concepts we've covered are the building blocks for a successful career and life. I've used them unconsciously with great success, and I've also used them consciously to reinvent and rebuild myself at the lowest point of my life. I have also passed these on to the many payroll professionals that we've trained, so it is with the utmost confidence that I encourage you to make this moment your turning point. Apply everything you've learned, take it one step at a time, and commit to seeing this through. Your future happiness, success, and fulfillment depend on you choosing to invest in yourself.

The Ever-Evolving Journey

Becoming a successful global payroll professional is a continuous journey, not a one-time achievement. It requires ongoing growth and development and a commitment to lead with courage, accountability, and a sense of social responsibility. Your journey as a payroll professional is a dynamic one, marked by the challenges you overcome, the influence you build, and the positive change you drive within your organization. As you embrace the role with a renewed spirit, keep in mind that it's not just a position; it's a path to becoming a force for good within your organization. Choose to embark on this journey that transcends job titles and brings with it the opportunity to create a lasting impact and contribute to the long-term success of your team and organization. It's an opportunity that, when approached with dedication and purpose, will make you not only a better leader but also a better human being.

The Evergreen Legacy of Influence

As you journey through your professional and personal life challenges, remember that influence is not about momentary success but rather a lasting legacy. The resilience and problem-solving skills you cultivate will continue to serve you well, contributing to your growth and influence for years to come. Remember my golfing analogy? I've come to appreciate the obstacles on the golf course as representing the challenges we must face in global payroll. These obstacles aren't there to drown or fail us but rather to be used as stepping stones so that we may rise to greater heights and make manifest our visions and dreams. Every challenge you overcome is a lesson, a chance to build your endurance, and a stepping stone on your path to becoming a more influential leader, team player, and human being. Your enduring legacy of influence, a sense of fulfillment, and a bright future in payroll start with the resilience you build today. Commit to your transformation. Expect nothing but the best for your future, and above all else, dare to be who you really are.

To your success,

Bart Van Der Storm.

Recommended Resources

Elevate yourself and continue stepping up your game as a payroll professional with the following resources:

Payrollmind DNA assessment

Take the assessment to identify your payroll profile and uncover opportunities for growth. You'll also gain access to insights and tips from me and my hand-picked expert talent consultants. Find it at *payrollminds.com/dna-assessment.*

Strategy session

Book a strategy session, where we'll use my transformative strategy framework to uncover opportunities to optimize your multi-country payroll. Visit *payrollminds.com* to request additional information.

Payrollminds newsletter

Sign up for the Payrollminds newsletter to receive our latest global payroll insights and activities in your inbox. Visit *payrollminds.com* to sign up.

Payrollminds LinkedIn

Follow Payrollminds on LinkedIn to join the conversation on redefining global payroll into a representation of work's true value. Find us at *linkedin.com/company/payrollminds/*.

Made in United States
North Haven, CT
17 April 2024